The Art of Emotional Alchemy:
Turning Negative Feelings into
Positive Energy

Kunya Ilm
(Self-Help Series)

The Art of Emotional Alchemy: Turning Negative Feelings into Positive Energy

1. The Alchemist's Secret: Transforming Your Emotions (Page 6)
2. From Lead to Gold: The Art of Emotional Alchemy (Page 14)
3. Uncovering the Magic: Discovering the Power of Emotional Alchemy (Page 22)
4. The Heart's Crucible: Turning Pain into Purpose (Page 27)
5. The Alchemist's Laboratory: Mixing Emotions with Intention (Page 30)
6. The Phoenix Principle: Rising from the Ashes of Negative Emotions (Page 37)
7. The Golden Thread: Weaving Positivity through Emotional Alchemy (Page 45)
8. The Spark of Change: Igniting Transformation in Your Emotions (Page 52)
9. The Alchemist's Toolbox: Tools for Transmuting Negative Emotions (Page 57)
10. The Mirror's Reflection: Facing Your Emotions Head-On (Page 66)

The Art of Emotional Alchemy: Turning Negative Feelings into Positive Energy

11. The Alchemist's Forge: Crafting Your Emotional Future (Page 72)
12. The Alchemy of Joy: Finding Happiness through Emotional Alchemy (Page 79)
13. The Alchemist's Elixir: Cultivating Emotional Wellness (Page 85)
14. The Alchemist's Wisdom: Insights for Navigating Your Emotions (Page 93)
15. The Art of Inner Alchemy: Transforming Your Inner Landscape (Page 98)
16. The Alchemist's Compass: Navigating the Terrain of Your Emotions (Page 103)
17. The Alchemist's Journey: A Path of Transformation (Page 108)
18. The Alchemy of Forgiveness: Healing Your Emotional Wounds (Page 113)
19. The Alchemy of Gratitude: Cultivating a Positive Mindset (Page 119)
20. The Alchemy of Love: Transmuting Negative Emotions into Love (Page 125)

The Art of Emotional Alchemy: Turning Negative Feelings into Positive Energy

21. The Alchemy of Creativity: Harnessing Your Emotions for Creative Inspiration (Page 130)
22. The Alchemy of Connection: Building Positive Relationships (Page 137)
23. The Alchemy of Self-Discovery: Exploring Your Inner World (Page 142)
24. The Alchemist's Legacy: Leaving a Positive Emotional Footprint (Page 148)
25. The Alchemy of Courage: Transforming Fear into Bravery (Page 152)
26. The Alchemy of Resilience: Bouncing Back from Emotional Setbacks (Page 161)
27. The Alchemist's Canvas: Painting Your Emotional Landscape (Page 165)
28. The Alchemy of Patience: Navigating Your Emotions with Grace (Page 169)
29. The Alchemy of Humility: Letting Go of Negative Emotions (Page 172)
30. The Alchemy of Trust: Building Trust with Yourself and Others (Page 177)

The Art of Emotional Alchemy: Turning Negative Feelings into Positive Energy

31. The Alchemy of Wisdom: Learning from Your Emotions (Page 182)
32. The Alchemy of Balance: Finding Equilibrium in Your Emotions (Page 187)
33. The Alchemy of Self-Love: Transforming Negative Self-Talk into Self-Love (Page 193)

*

The Art of Emotional Alchemy: Turning Negative Feelings into Positive Energy

The Alchemist's Secret: Transforming Your Emotions

Dealing with our emotions is one of the most difficult components of the search for self-discovery. Until we learn how to change them, our feelings can be like the elusive material used by the alchemist; we never really know what they will do or how they will affect us. The process of transformation is the key to alchemy, and it is through the alteration of our emotions that we can start to comprehend the innermost parts of ourselves.

As highly complex beings, humans experience a wide spectrum of emotions, including happiness, sadness, rage, fear, and surprise. These feelings can be crippling and oftentimes overwhelming. They may skew our judgement, harm our relationships, and make it harder for us to accomplish our objectives. The fact that so many people struggle with their emotions and look for ways to change them is understandable.

The Art of Emotional Alchemy: Turning Negative Feelings into Positive Energy

The good news is that altering our emotions is not only feasible, but also essential for happiness and personal development. Really, the secret to realising our potential and leading a satisfying life is to modify our emotions. So how do we change our feelings? The solution can be found in a few fundamental techniques that call for perseverance, commitment, and a readiness to delve into the core of who we are.

Accept Your Feelings

Fully embracing your feelings is the first step towards transforming them. Trying to repress or dismiss our emotions will only make them worse because they are a natural part of who we are. Instead, we should be aware of, accepting, and understanding the sources of our emotions.

No matter how uncomfortable our feelings may be, we must give ourselves permission to experience them.

The Art of Emotional Alchemy: Turning Negative Feelings into Positive Energy

"Emotions cannot be controlled. How you handle them is." - Mark Brackett

Recognize the root cause

Understanding the source of our feelings comes when we have accepted them. Every feeling we experience has a cause, and once we can pinpoint that cause, we can start to work on changing the way we feel. In order to do this, we must examine our past experiences, beliefs, and ideals while also being honest with ourselves.

"There is more clarity the better you understand yourself. Self-awareness has no bounds." - J. Krishnamurti

The Art of Emotional Alchemy: Turning Negative Feelings into Positive Energy

Exercise Self-Reflection

Self-reflection is a potent technique for changing our feelings. It enables us to distance ourselves from our emotions and thoughts so that we may view them objectively. By doing this, we can spot patterns in our actions, attitudes, and feelings and start to comprehend how they are related. In order to complete this process, we must be mindful of our feelings and thoughts and observe them objectively.

"Understanding oneself is the beginning of all wisdom."
– Aristotle

Develop mindfulness

Another effective strategy for managing our emotions is mindfulness. It entails being in the present moment and monitoring our thoughts and sensations with an impartial

The Art of Emotional Alchemy: Turning Negative Feelings into Positive Energy

and open mind. Being mindful enables us to step back from our emotions and watch them as they change throughout time. We can learn to respond to our emotions rather than simply react to them by doing this.

"Mindfulness is simple; all we need to do is remember to practise it." Sharon Salzberg

Employ uplifting statements.

We may change our emotions by using positive affirmations, which are a powerful tool. They entail telling ourselves encouraging things over and over again to bolster our optimistic thoughts and combat negative self-talk. We may rewire our subconscious minds and change our emotions by repeating affirmations that are positive.

The Art of Emotional Alchemy: Turning Negative Feelings into Positive Energy

Cultivate gratitude

Another effective technique for altering our emotions is practising thankfulness. It entails emphasising and expressing thankfulness for the good things in our lives. By doing this, we reorient our attention away from our unpleasant feelings and towards the things that make us happy and joyful. Gratitude exercises can help us change our emotions and develop a happy mindset.

"Gratitude provides a vision for the future, brings serenity to the present, and makes sense of our past." - Melanie Beattie

Exercise Self-Care

For us to change our emotions, self-care is crucial. Our physical, emotional, and mental health must all be taken into consideration. Taking care of oneself can take many different forms, including getting adequate sleep, eating

The Art of Emotional Alchemy: Turning Negative Feelings into Positive Energy

well, exercising frequently, and making time for our favourite activities. We can lower our stress levels, lift our spirits, and rewire our emotions by engaging in self-care.

"It is possible to nourish yourself in a way that enables you to develop in the direction you want to go, and you are worth the effort." - Debbie Day

Seek Assistance

It can be difficult to change our feelings, so it's crucial to get help from others. This person might be a friend, relative, therapist, or coach. Discussing our feelings with others can give us fresh viewpoints and insights as well as the support and inspiration we need to keep moving forwards in our transformational process.

"Support, motivation, and encouragement are needed by everyone." Kristian Kan

The Art of Emotional Alchemy: Turning Negative Feelings into Positive Energy

In conclusion, changing our emotions is a crucial part of developing personally and finding pleasure. We may modify our emotions and reach our full potential by embracing them, comprehending their underlying causes, engaging in self-reflection and mindfulness, utilising positive affirmations, taking care of ourselves, and reaching out for help. Being patient, gentle, and compassionate with yourself along the way is important since transformation is a journey rather than a destination.

*

The Art of Emotional Alchemy: Turning Negative Feelings into Positive Energy

From Lead to Gold: The Art of Emotional Alchemy

Emotions are a strong force that can either advance us or hold us back. Our emotions might occasionally feel like lead, weighing us down and depleting our energy. But, with the correct methods and techniques, we can change our feelings from negative to positive, transforming our suffering into strength and our weaknesses into assets. This process, known as emotional alchemy, is a profound art that has the power to unleash our potential and effect long-lasting transformation in our lives.

"Emotional alchemy is the transforming of base emotions into emotions that nourish the soul." - Tara Brach

The Art of Emotional Alchemy: Turning Negative Feelings into Positive Energy

The Alchemy of Kindness

Our emotions can be changed from sour to sweet by the powerful emotion of compassion. By having compassion for ourselves and others, we are recognising our shared humanity and intrinsic value. This perspective change can aid in the development of an understanding and empathy that can promote healing and progress.

Treating ourselves with compassion and understanding, despite our shortcomings and imperfections, is a key component of self-compassion practice. Embracing self-acceptance and letting go of self-criticism are required for this. We may improve our resilience and adaptability as well as change our negative emotions into positive ones when we practise self-compassion.

"Self-compassion is simply giving the same kindness to ourselves that we would give to others." - Christopher Germer

The Art of Emotional Alchemy: Turning Negative Feelings into Positive Energy

The Alchemy of Forgiveness

We can let go of the burden of our previous grudges and resentments with the help of the transformative feeling of forgiveness. When we harbour resentments and grudges, we are carrying a heavy load that can drag us down and keep us from finding happiness and fulfilment. But when we decide to forgive ourselves and others, we may make room for recovery and development.

Giving up the want for vengeance or retaliation and deciding to show compassion and understanding are both necessary components of forgiveness. This is letting go of the emotional charge and making progress in the direction of peace and resolution rather than tolerating destructive behaviour or forgetting the past.

The Art of Emotional Alchemy: Turning Negative Feelings into Positive Energy

By choosing forgiveness, we can change our negative feelings of resentment and anger into positive ones like empathy and understanding.

"Forgiveness is not an occasional act, it is a constant attitude." - Martin Luther King Jr.

The Alchemy of Authenticity

Authenticity is a potent emotion that can assist us in converting our gloomy feelings of fear and self-doubt into radiant ones of self-assurance and self-expression. When we embrace who we truly are, we are honouring our special abilities and talents as well as our intrinsic worth. This change of viewpoint can aid us in developing a sense of self-worth and self-esteem, which can give us the confidence to take chances and go for our aspirations.

The Art of Emotional Alchemy: Turning Negative Feelings into Positive Energy

Being authentic means staying true to who we are and speaking out bravely and honestly about our views and feelings. This entails choosing to follow our own inner compass rather than trying to please others or live up to social norms. When we accept who we truly are, we may change our gloomy feelings of fear and self-doubt into radiant ones of courage and assurance.

"Authenticity is the daily practice of letting go of who we think we're supposed to be and embracing who we are." - Brené Brown

The Alchemy of Happiness

Experiencing joy can help us change our perspective from one of scarcity to one of abundance. When we practise joy, we stop focusing on our issues and limits and instead appreciate the opportunities and benefits in our lives. This perspective change can have a significant

The Art of Emotional Alchemy: Turning Negative Feelings into Positive Energy

impact on our emotional state since it encourages us to develop feelings of happiness, contentment, and thankfulness.

Embracing the present moment and appreciating life's little joys are key components of practising joy. This entails letting go of the demand for excellence or perpetual striving and deciding to be grateful for what we already have. As we practise joy, we can change our gloomy, hopeless emotions into radiant ones of thankfulness and optimism.

"Joy is what happens to us when we allow ourselves to recognize how good things really are." - Marianne Williamson

The Art of Emotional Alchemy: Turning Negative Feelings into Positive Energy

The Alchemy of Fortitude

We can overcome challenges and overcome adversity by using the transformational emotion of resilience. When we practise resilience, we are honouring our inner strength and the fact that we are capable of overcoming even the most daunting obstacles.

This perspective change can assist us in developing a spirit of bravery and resolve that will enable us to more easily deal with life's ups and downs.

Resilience training entails accepting failure's lessons and using them as stepping stones to achievement. This entails letting go of the fear of failure and deciding to perceive failures as chances for growth and learning.

The Art of Emotional Alchemy: Turning Negative Feelings into Positive Energy

As we practise resilience, we can change our gloomy feelings of defeat and despair into radiant ones of tenacity and fortitude.

"The greatest glory in living lies not in never falling, but in rising every time we fall." - Nelson Mandela

In conclusion, the profound technique of emotional alchemy can help us turn our sour feelings into sweet ones. We can reach our greatest potential and bring about long-lasting change in our lives by fostering compassion, forgiveness, authenticity, joy, and resilience. Patience, practise, and a readiness to accept our frailties and flaws are necessary for this process. But, emotional alchemy has enormous benefits since it can make our lives more honest and rewarding.

"The alchemy of life is to turn lead into gold. The alchemy of emotions is to transform our base emotions into emotions that nourish the soul." - Robin S. Sharma

The Art of Emotional Alchemy: Turning Negative Feelings into Positive Energy

Uncovering the Magic: Discovering the Power of Emotional Alchemy

The art of turning negative emotions into pleasant ones is known as emotional alchemy. It's similar to converting lead into gold, but the transition is psychological rather than physical. The human experience is not complete without emotions, which are also very strong. Depending on how we handle things, they can either help us or hurt us.

The secret to emotional alchemy is our capacity to change our viewpoint and view things from a different angle. Although we often have no control over what happens to us, we do have influence over how we respond. We can manage our emotions and make positive changes in our lives thanks to the alchemy of emotions.

The Art of Emotional Alchemy: Turning Negative Feelings into Positive Energy

Scenario One:

Consider that you recently lost your job. You feel frustrated, helpless, and lost. You can decide to turn those negative feelings into positive ones, or you can decide to stay in that negative state and wallow in self-pity.

You can start by being kind towards yourself. It's important to recognise that losing a job is a big loss. In this trying time, take care of yourself and be gentle to yourself.

Next, work on forgiving others. Forgive yourself, forgive your old employer, and forgive the circumstance. Hanging onto your rage and grudges won't make things better and will just make you feel worse. You may move on and let go of the unpleasant feelings when you forgive.

The Art of Emotional Alchemy: Turning Negative Feelings into Positive Energy

Next, put authenticity first. Spend some time deciding what you truly want from your future professional move. Use this as a chance to discover new avenues and land a career that fits with your values and passions.

Lastly, practise resilience. Keep in mind that failure is OK and that setbacks are a normal part of life. Make use of this experience as a stepping stone to further development and advancement. Have confidence in your capacity to solve this challenge.

Scenario Two:

Consider yourself in a failing relationship. You feel unhappy, stuck, and frustrated. You have the option of either continuing to suffer while remaining in that negative environment or choosing to change those negative feelings into happy ones.

The Art of Emotional Alchemy: Turning Negative Feelings into Positive Energy

Start by being compassionate towards both yourself and your relationship. Recognizing that relationships can be difficult is important. During this trying period, be gentle to yourself and your partner.

Next, work on forgiving others. Forgive your partner, yourself, and the circumstance. Hanging onto your rage and grudges won't make things better and will just make you feel worse. You may move on and let go of the unpleasant feelings when you forgive.

Next, put authenticity first. Spend some time determining what you truly desire in a relationship. Find a partner who shares your beliefs and aspirations by using this as an opportunity to explore your wants and desires.

Lastly, practise resilience. Keep in mind that relationships are complicated, and it's good to experience difficulties.

The Art of Emotional Alchemy: Turning Negative Feelings into Positive Energy

Make the most of this experience as a chance to learn and develop personally. Have faith in your abilities to discover pleasure and fulfilment.

A potent technique that enables us to change unfavourable feelings into favourable ones is emotional alchemy. We may bring about positive change in our lives by cultivating compassion, forgiveness, sincerity, and resilience. Patience, practise, and a readiness to accept vulnerability and flaws are necessary for this process. But, emotional alchemy has enormous benefits since it can make our lives more honest and rewarding.

Alchemy involves more than just turning lead into gold. You have the ability to change negative things into positive ones, such as turning pain into joy or fear into love. Emotional alchemy's genuine magic lies in this.

*

The Art of Emotional Alchemy: Turning Negative Feelings into Positive Energy

The Heart's Crucible: Turning Pain into Purpose

Throughout life, grief and heartache are universal experiences. It is a necessary component of the human experience. But how we handle that suffering can really make a difference. The crucible of the heart is a metaphor for the process of transforming our suffering into meaning. It's about taking our challenges and using them to improve the world for the better.

Recognizing and accepting our sorrow is the first step in transforming it into purpose. We can't proceed until we've properly acknowledged and dealt with our pain. Although this process might be challenging and uncomfortable, it is essential for development and healing.

We can begin to investigate our pain once we've acknowledged it. What can I learn from this experience, for example, is a question we can pose to ourselves.

The Art of Emotional Alchemy: Turning Negative Feelings into Positive Energy

Also, how can I make use of this suffering to assist others? This investigation may enable us to comprehend ourselves and our purpose more fully.

The work of novelist and activist Jennifer Storm, who has devoted her life to aiding others in recovering from addiction and trauma, is one example of how sorrow may be turned into purpose. Jennifer's memoir "Blackout Girl," which has assisted countless others who have experienced similar challenges, was motivated by her own battles with addiction and sexual abuse.

Another illustration is Malala Yousafzai's efforts, who was assassinated by the Taliban for supporting girls' education. Malala channelled her suffering into ensuring that every girl has access to school, rather than letting it keep her from speaking. Her tenacity and bravery have motivated millions of people all across the world.

The Art of Emotional Alchemy: Turning Negative Feelings into Positive Energy

Transforming grief into purpose can have transforming effects on both the self and others. We not only help ourselves by using our challenges to make the world a better place, but we also change it when we do.

In summary, the heart's crucible serves as a potent metaphor for the process of transforming suffering into meaning. We can make our problems meaningful by recognising and accepting our pain, exploring it, and using it to bring about constructive change. The lives of Malala Yousafzai and Jennifer Storm serve as examples of how we can use our suffering to change the world. So let's accept our suffering, grow from it, and use it to improve the world.

"Out of suffering have emerged the strongest souls; the most massive characters are seared with scars." - Khalil Gibran
"Your pain is the breaking of the shell that encloses your understanding." - Kahlil Gibran

The Art of Emotional Alchemy: Turning Negative Feelings into Positive Energy

The Alchemist's Laboratory: Mixing Emotions with Intention

Emotions and intentions are combined in the alchemist's laboratory to produce transformational effects. The emotional alchemist must be deliberate and exact in their approach to emotional transformation, just as a scientist meticulously weighs and blends ingredients to generate a desired response.

To start, it's critical to understand that emotions are strong forces that can significantly affect our lives. Negative emotions can trigger self-destructive behaviour, strained relationships, and even physical health issues if they are not managed. Nonetheless, we may use the strength of our emotions to accomplish our goals and lead fulfilling lives if we can learn to control them.

Becoming conscious of our emotions is the first step in the emotional alchemy process. Learning to recognise

The Art of Emotional Alchemy: Turning Negative Feelings into Positive Energy

and label the emotions we are feeling is necessary for this. It's critical to keep in mind that every emotion, including the unpleasant ones, serves a function. We can start to work with our emotions rather than against them by recognising and accepting them.

Setting intentions for our emotional change is the next phase. This entails being explicit about our objectives and establishing objectives that are consistent with our values and aspirations. For instance, if we have a hard time controlling our wrath, we could want to practise showing others greater tolerance and compassion.

Once we have recognised our feelings and established our goals, we may start combining them in the alchemist's pot. This entails utilising a variety of instruments and methods to convert our feelings into something beneficial and useful. The use of a therapist or coach, journaling, mindfulness meditation, or creative expression are a few of these methods.

The Art of Emotional Alchemy: Turning Negative Feelings into Positive Energy

Visualisation is a potent technique for transforming emotions. This includes visualising the desired result in our minds through the power of imagination. For instance, if we wish to increase our self-confidence, we can picture ourselves getting through a difficult scenario or accomplishing a long-term objective. We can start to rewire our brains and develop new neural connections that support our emotional transformation by routinely envisioning the outcomes we want.

Self-compassion is a key component of emotional alchemy. It's crucial to treat ourselves with kindness and gentleness as we undergo the process of emotional development. This entails accepting our flaws and errors without condemnation or criticism of ourselves. We can create a welcoming and nurturing atmosphere for our emotional development by being kind and compassionate to ourselves.

The Art of Emotional Alchemy: Turning Negative Feelings into Positive Energy

Emotions and intentions are like chemicals in the alchemist's lab, mixing in different ways to produce novel and transformational effects. We can transform unpleasant emotions into positive ones, develop new virtues and strengths, and accomplish our objectives and aspirations by taking an intentional and purposeful approach to emotional transformation.

Carl Jung once said, "What you fight, persists," which is a sensible statement that relates to emotional alchemy. This implies that our bad emotions will still have control over us if we try to ignore them or push them away. But, if we can learn to accept and manage our emotions, we may use them to our advantage and turn them into something constructive.

The poet Rumi also said, "The wound is the spot where the light enters you," which is another insightful statement. This supports the premise that our emotional metamorphosis can be sparked by our grief and

The Art of Emotional Alchemy: Turning Negative Feelings into Positive Energy

hardships. We may transform our pain into purpose and bring about positive change in our life and the world around us by accepting our scars and drawing inspiration from them.

Here are two scenarios encapsulating the very premise of the core concept of mixing emotion with intention:

Scenario One:

Entrepreneur Jennifer has worked hard to go up the corporate ladder. She has always felt dissatisfied and cut off from her work despite her accomplishments. She struggles to find significance in her everyday activities and frequently feels stressed, anxious, and overburdened. She makes the decision to experiment with emotional alchemy one day.

She starts to pay attention to her feelings and practises mindfulness so that she may observe them unperturbed.

The Art of Emotional Alchemy: Turning Negative Feelings into Positive Energy

She understands that the cause of her stress and worry is a misalignment with her genuine values and purpose. She discovers her love for social justice via self-reflection and decides to pursue a job in the non-profit sector. She discovers the sense of fulfilment and purpose she had been missing when she matches her profession with her principles and hobbies.

Scenario Two:

John, a college student, recently underwent a challenging split. He is distraught and overcome with emotion. He struggles to concentrate on his schoolwork and is frequently agitated and depressed. He is advised by a buddy to experiment with emotional alchemy. John begins by recognising his feelings and investigating the ideas and preconceptions that underlie them. He understands that his sorrow has been prolonged by his holding onto restrictive notions about himself and his deserving.

The Art of Emotional Alchemy: Turning Negative Feelings into Positive Energy

He chooses to confront these beliefs and swap them out for more powerful ones using the cognitive restructuring technique. He starts to turn his attention away from the hurt of the split and onto the chances for development and education it offers. Also, he starts giving self-care routines like exercise, meditation, and journaling a higher priority. He gradually starts to feel more grounded and in control of himself as he employs these skills and strategies, and he is then better equipped to move forwards with clarity and resilience.

The alchemist's laboratory is a place where feelings and intentions combine to yield transforming effects, to conclude. We can transform unpleasant emotions into positive ones, build new strengths and virtues, and accomplish our objectives and desires by approaching emotional transformation with intention, awareness, and self-compassion.

*

The Art of Emotional Alchemy: Turning Negative Feelings into Positive Energy

The Phoenix Principle: Rising from the Ashes of Negative Emotions

Although experiencing negative emotions can be excruciatingly unpleasant, they can also be a catalyst for change and development. We can use our bad emotions as fuel for our own personal development when we learn to alchemize them. We will look into the Phoenix Principle in this chapter, which teaches us to rise above our negative emotions and welcome our own rebirth.

The fabled bird known as the Phoenix is thought to resurrect from the ruins of its own demise. This bird is a potent representation of change and rebirth, and it teaches us that even the most trying circumstances can serve as the catalyst for our own growth.

The Phoenix Principle informs us that we can evolve via the utilisation of our negative emotions. We have a choice when we feel unpleasant emotions like anger,

The Art of Emotional Alchemy: Turning Negative Feelings into Positive Energy

sadness, or fear. Either we can let these feelings overwhelm us or we can let them fuel our own development. We can rise from the ashes of our bad experiences and become stronger and more resilient than ever before by embracing our emotions and learning from them.

Self-compassion is one of the Phoenix Principle's main instruments. It might be simple to slip into self-criticism and self-judgement when we feel bad. We may hold ourselves accountable for our feelings or feel guilty for having them in the first place. Yet, self-compassion helps us to accept, understand, and be kind to ourselves. We can start to learn from our emotions without condemnation or self-blame if we approach them with self-compassion.

Reframing is another useful Phoenix Principle tool. The process of reframing involves altering the way we see our unpleasant experiences. We can learn to perceive our

The Art of Emotional Alchemy: Turning Negative Feelings into Positive Energy

emotions as possibilities for development and learning rather than something to be avoided or hidden. Such inquiries as "What can I learn from this experience?" and "How can I use this feeling to fuel my personal evolution?" might be asked of ourselves. By changing the way we think about our unpleasant experiences, we can start to see them as learning opportunities rather than challenges to overcome.

The Phoenix Principle likewise encourages us to live in the present. It can be simple to get sucked into the past or the future when we are feeling bad. We could obsess over past errors or fret about unknowns in the future. We may, however, learn to accept our feelings and draw lessons from them in the here and now by keeping our attention on the present. We can enquire about ourselves, "What am I feeling at this moment?" or "What can I learn from this emotion at this time?" We can learn to alchemize our emotions and use them as fuel for our own personal development by remaining present with them.

The Art of Emotional Alchemy: Turning Negative Feelings into Positive Energy

The account of Ruth Bader Ginsburg serves as an illustration of the Phoenix Principle in action. Throughout her life, Ginsburg had to overcome many difficulties and barriers, including prejudice, illness, and loss. She made the decision to use these encounters as a catalyst for personal development and global change, nevertheless. "Real change, enduring change, happens one step at a time," she once said. Ginsburg was able to rise above her painful past and turn into a potent force for change and advancement by accepting the Phoenix Principle.

Nelson Mandela's life narrative serves as another illustration of the Phoenix Principle in action. Mandela was imprisoned for 27 years because he opposed apartheid in South Africa. He was determined not to let this incident define him, though. Instead, he made the most of his incarceration to think, grow, and learn.

The Art of Emotional Alchemy: Turning Negative Feelings into Positive Energy

He was transformed upon his release from prison, with a strong sense of purpose and a dedication to justice and equality. I discovered that courage, in his own words, "was not the absence of fear, but the triumph over it."

Integrating the Phoenix Principle into our life entails accepting the transformational process and realising the influence of our unfavourable emotions. It entails allowing oneself to experience the suffering, accepting it, and then letting it serve as a springboard for development.

Nothing comes without pain, as the saying goes. We must be willing to face and work through our negative feelings if we are to rise above them. Although this procedure can be challenging and uncomfortable, it is eventually required. By doing this, we can become more resilient, wiser, and strong than before.

The Art of Emotional Alchemy: Turning Negative Feelings into Positive Energy

Reframing our unpleasant experiences is a crucial component of the Phoenix Principle. We might decide to perceive them as chances for development and transformation rather than as setbacks or failures. What doesn't kill you only makes you stronger, as the philosopher Friedrich Nietzsche once stated. By adopting this attitude, we can leverage our suffering to propel change for the better.

The Phoenix Principle also emphasises the importance of self-compassion. It's critical to keep in mind that because we are all human, we will undoubtedly make errors and feel pain. Self-compassion means treating oneself with kindness and understanding rather than criticising or concentrating on our shortcomings. Thich Nhat Hanh, a Buddhist teacher, famously said: "Being authentic is the key to being beautiful. You're not dependent on other people's approval. You must accept who you are."

The Art of Emotional Alchemy: Turning Negative Feelings into Positive Energy

Creating a "transformational toolbox" full of methods and approaches for overcoming negative emotions is one realistic way to apply the Phoenix Principle to our life. Journaling, meditation, mindfulness, exercise, counselling, and conversations with close friends and family members are a few tools that could be in this toolbox.

Imagine, for instance, that you just went through a heartbreaking breakup. You could apply the Phoenix Principle to turn your suffering into purpose rather than dwell in your melancholy and despair. Start by giving yourself permission to feel your emotions and grieve. The separation could then be reframed as a chance for growth and personal development. You might also use this experience to discover more about who you are, what you want in a partner, or to discover new interests and hobbies.

The Art of Emotional Alchemy: Turning Negative Feelings into Positive Energy

You could also seek assistance from your transformational toolkit. Perhaps you find that writing in a notebook or doing meditation helps you feel more grounded and centred. You can progressively work through your suffering and come out stronger and more resilient by employing these techniques.

The Phoenix Principle provides a potent paradigm for converting our unfavourable emotions into sources of development and resilience, to recap. We can rise from the ashes of our suffering and become more resilient and entire than we were before by accepting the process of transformation, reinterpreting our traumatic experiences, and cultivating self-compassion. Inevitably, we may create space for healing, development, and transformation by allowing ourselves to experience and work through our pain.

*

The Art of Emotional Alchemy: Turning Negative Feelings into Positive Energy

The Golden Thread: Weaving Positivity through Emotional Alchemy

We have looked at the practice of emotional alchemy and how it might change our unfavourable feelings into favourable ones. But it's equally crucial to foster optimism in our life and include it into our routine of daily emotional alchemy. Our lives are woven together with positivity, which serves as a golden thread linking us to our higher selves and directing us towards a life of meaning and fulfilment.

Being positive is a manner of being rather than just a state of thought. It is the capacity to find the positive in every circumstance, to remain hopeful and joyful in the face of hardship, and to exude love and generosity towards those who are close to us. Positive thinking is contagious and has the capacity to boost others around us, having a wide-reaching ripple impact.

The Art of Emotional Alchemy: Turning Negative Feelings into Positive Energy

So how can we incorporate optimism into our emotional alchemy practise? Here are a few methods:

Gratitude:

Expressing gratitude is an effective way to foster optimism. We change our attention from what is lacking to what is abundant in our life when we concentrate on what we are grateful for. Gratitude makes it possible for us to recognise the beauty in each moment and to value the people and situations that make us happy. Whether it's through journaling, meditation, or just pausing for a moment to think about your blessings, make it a habit to practise thankfulness every day.

"In order to carry out a positive action, we must develop a positive vision." - Dalai Lama

The Art of Emotional Alchemy: Turning Negative Feelings into Positive Energy

Positive Affirmations:

Affirmations are effective methods for retraining our brains and fostering positivity. Positive affirmations help us develop a positive outlook on life and self-belief by repeatedly reinforcing them in our brains. Make a list of affirmations that speak to you and say them to yourself or aloud to yourself every day.

"Positive anything is better than negative nothing." - Elbert Hubbard

Implementation of Positivity:

Positivity is important to surround yourself with since it has a significant impact on your mental health. Look for people who are upbeat, encouraging, and who encourage you to grow and be your best. Whether it be through art,

The Art of Emotional Alchemy: Turning Negative Feelings into Positive Energy

music, or nature, create spaces that make you happy and peaceful.

"Positive thinking will let you do everything better than negative thinking will." - Zig Ziglar

Acts of kindness:

When we do kind things for others, we feel happier ourselves. Find ways to have a positive influence wherever you go, whether it be with a smile, a kind word, or a helpful act. Kindnesses have a contagious effect that can change the world.

"Positive anything is better than negative nothing." - Elbert Hubbard

The Art of Emotional Alchemy: Turning Negative Feelings into Positive Energy

Living Mindfully:

Living mindfully means paying close attention to the current moment without passing judgement or getting distracted. Living thoughtfully cultivates an inner sense of calm and optimism that spills out into the world. Use mindfulness in your daily activities, whether it be through meditation, attentive breathing, or just being aware of the moment.

"The most important thing is to try and inspire people so that they can be great in whatever they want to do." - Kobe Bryant

To sum up, emotional alchemy is the act of changing unfavourable feelings into favourable ones, or turning lead into gold. It is a talent that can be developed through practice in order to lead a happier and more satisfying life. We can learn to recognise our emotions, comprehend them, and change them into beneficial

The Art of Emotional Alchemy: Turning Negative Feelings into Positive Energy

experiences by applying the concepts of emotional alchemy. We can discover the magic within ourselves, turn our pain into purpose, and emerge from the ashes of our negative emotions like a phoenix.

Emotional alchemy is not a quick fix or a one-time treatment. It calls for persistent work and a readiness to compassionately and genuinely investigate our feelings. It is a lifelong path that can ultimately result in a more contented and meaningful life by fostering a greater awareness of both oneself and others.

"The art of alchemy is simply the skill of becoming oneself," once declared the prominent philosopher and alchemist Paracelsus. We have the chance to become the finest versions of ourselves by embracing emotional alchemy, turning our stale feelings into precious chances for development and transformation.

The Art of Emotional Alchemy: Turning Negative Feelings into Positive Energy

So let's employ emotional alchemy, one emotion at a time, to weave a golden thread of optimism through our lives. Recall the strength of our goals, the alchemy of our hearts, and the magic that resides within each and every one of us.

*

The Art of Emotional Alchemy: Turning Negative Feelings into Positive Energy

The Spark of Change: Igniting Transformation in Your Emotions

Life's only constant is change. When we move through various stages of our lives, it is normal for us to feel a variety of emotions. But it's important to understand that how we handle these feelings can have a big impact on our mental and emotional health.

A potent technique that might assist us in igniting change in our emotions is emotional alchemy. It permits us to alter how we perceive unpleasant feelings and turn them into enjoyable experiences. We can lead happier, more fulfilled lives if we can learn to control our emotions.

We must first acknowledge the spark within us in order to start a transformation in our emotions.

The Art of Emotional Alchemy: Turning Negative Feelings into Positive Energy

The spark stands for our innate power, enthusiasm, and drive for change. It is the light that leads us out of the shadows and gives us the power to change our feelings.

There are numerous methods to light the spark of transformation. Some people may be affected by a traumatic experience or a major life event. Others could experience it as a gradual process of personal development. Whatever the spark's origin, it is crucial to acknowledge and welcome it.

The greatest discovery of my generation, according to the eminent psychologist and philosopher William James, is that a person may change his life by changing his attitudes. The spark of change indicates our attitude towards our emotions. We can cause change in our emotions by altering our attitude.

By altering our internal dialogue, we can spark change in our emotions. The internal conversation we have with

The Art of Emotional Alchemy: Turning Negative Feelings into Positive Energy

ourselves is referred to as self-talk. It can have a big impact on our emotional health and can be either positive or negative. We may modify our emotions and produce a more positive experience by switching from negative to positive self-talk.

Imagine, for instance, that you are in a circumstance where you are feeling a negative emotion, like rage or irritation. If so, you can alter your internal dialogue by telling yourself that these feelings are fleeting and that you have the ability to turn them into a positive experience. You may start the transformation within you and produce a happier emotional state by altering your self-talk.

Gratitude exercises are another approach to trigger emotional development. The act of being grateful for what we have in life is known as gratitude.
It is a potent tool that can assist us in turning our attention away from what we lack and towards what we

The Art of Emotional Alchemy: Turning Negative Feelings into Positive Energy

do have. We can cultivate a more pleasant emotional state and start the transformation of our emotions by practising appreciation.

Consider being in a depressive or sad mood as an example of a negative emotional state. Next you can practise gratitude by thinking back on the good things in your life, such as your health, your family, or your job. You can start a transformation within yourself and develop a more optimistic emotional state by cultivating appreciation.

According to Tony Robbins, a well-known author and motivational speaker, "Change comes when the pain of staying the same is greater than the pain of change." The willingness to accept the discomfort of change and transform our emotions is symbolised by the spark of change.

The Art of Emotional Alchemy: Turning Negative Feelings into Positive Energy

Ultimately, the key to igniting change in our emotions is the spark of change. We may design a more satisfying and joyous existence by acknowledging the spark within us, altering our self-talk, cultivating gratitude, and accepting the discomfort of change. "As above, so below, as within, so without, as the universe, so the soul," as the ancient alchemists used to say. We can change our emotions to make ourselves feel better, which will then make the world around us feel better as well.

*

The Art of Emotional Alchemy: Turning Negative Feelings into Positive Energy

The Alchemist's Toolbox: Tools for Transmuting Negative Emotions

Our human experience is fundamentally shaped by our emotions, although they may become overwhelming and challenging to control. The good news is that there are methods and strategies we may employ to assist in transforming unfavourable feelings into favourable ones. We can employ a variety of methods to change our emotions, just as an alchemist utilises a variety of instruments to turn base metals into gold. We'll look at some of the best methods for emotional alchemy in this chapter.

Initial Tool: Mindfulness

Being aware is among the most effective methods for transforming emotions. The practice of mindfulness entails being in the present moment while objectively monitoring our thoughts and emotions.

The Art of Emotional Alchemy: Turning Negative Feelings into Positive Energy

We can develop awareness of our emotions and develop more effective coping mechanisms by engaging in mindfulness practices.

A wise man once said, "Mindfulness is a method of becoming friends with ourselves and our experience." by Jon Kabat-Zinn

As an illustration, picture yourself experiencing anxiety before a presentation at work. You can learn to monitor your nervous thoughts without passing judgement and realise that they are simply that—thoughts—and not necessarily facts. The next step is to decide whether to keep your attention on the present while taking deep breaths and reminding yourself of your knowledge and experience.

"When we are no longer able to change a situation, we are challenged to change ourselves." - Viktor Frankl

The Art of Emotional Alchemy: Turning Negative Feelings into Positive Energy

Further explanation can be seen in the following scenario:

Sarah has battled anxiety for years and has tried a number of drugs and treatments without much results. She recently began mindfulness meditation, which has given her more awareness of and control over her worried thoughts and sensations. In order to analyse her feelings and get insight into her thought and behaviour patterns, she has also started keeping a notebook. Sarah is gradually learning how to use these methods to transform her worry into a source of strength and resilience.

Second Tool: Appreciation

Another effective instrument for emotional alchemy is gratitude. By concentrating on what we have to be thankful for, we turn our attention from negative to positive feelings.

The Art of Emotional Alchemy: Turning Negative Feelings into Positive Energy

Also, gratitude encourages us to have a more upbeat attitude on life, which can lower stress and enhance our general wellbeing.

The greatest virtue, and the parent of all others, is gratitude, according to this wise proverb. – Cicero

Consider the following scenario: You are annoyed because you have to work on a Saturday. By being grateful, you can concentrate on the fact that you have a job that pays you a regular salary and enables you to support your family. You could also be glad for the chance to develop and learn.

Third Tool: Compassion for Oneself

Being kinder and more forgiving to ourselves can be accomplished with the aid of self-compassion. Negative emotions are frequently fostered by self-judgement and

The Art of Emotional Alchemy: Turning Negative Feelings into Positive Energy

self-criticism. Through self-compassion exercises, we can develop the ability to treat ourselves with the same compassion and understanding that we would extend to a friend.

A wise person once said, "Self-compassion is just showing ourselves the same kindness that we would show others." A. Christopher Germer

Visualise a scenario, you made a mistake at work that cost the business money. You may accept that you are not perfect and that everyone makes errors by engaging in self-compassion exercises.
Then you can reaffirm your abilities and qualities and resolve to improve moving forwards by taking what you've learned to heart.

The Art of Emotional Alchemy: Turning Negative Feelings into Positive Energy

Fourth Tool: Exercise

Activity releases endorphins, which are known to naturally elevate mood. This makes exercise a potent weapon for emotional alchemy. Exercise can enhance our general sense of wellbeing and reduce stress and anxiety.

"Exercise is the path to a healthy mind and body," is a wise statement made by Rick Simmons.

For example, if you are furious and upset following a challenging talk with a relative. You may get rid of some of that stored up energy and elevate your mood by going for a run or engaging in some other sort of exercise. Exercise might also assist you in gaining perspective and generating useful answers.

Further explanation can be seen in the following scenario:

The Art of Emotional Alchemy: Turning Negative Feelings into Positive Energy

David has experienced issues in both his personal and professional lives as a result of his short fuse. Yet he only lately realised the value of working out as a good way to let pent-up emotions out. He works out or goes for a run whenever he feels his aggravation or rage building up, which helps him let off steam and gain more perspective. David is learning to regulate his bad emotions rather than letting them overtake him thanks to this new tool in his toolkit.

Fifth Tool: Creativity

We can use creative expression as a means to express our feelings in a healthy way. With writing, drawing, or music, for example, we can get insight into our thoughts and feelings and process our emotions.

Creative expression can be employed in the process of emotional alchemy. Creative expression, whether it be

The Art of Emotional Alchemy: Turning Negative Feelings into Positive Energy

through writing, painting, music, or any other form of art, can aid in the healthy processing and release of our emotions. Also, it can assist us in developing our inner knowledge and intuition, which can direct us towards greater emotional clarity and change.

Last but not least, it's critical to keep in mind the role that self-compassion plays in emotional alchemy. It's simple to fall victim to self-blame or self-criticism when we're coping with challenging emotions. These negative self-talk patterns, however, simply serve to keep us rooted in our suffering and prohibit us from making progress. We can learn to treat ourselves kindly, sympathetically, and supportively by developing self-compassion.

Thich Nhat Hanh, a Buddhist teacher, said: "A verb is compassion. It entails taking action." We can turn our negative emotions into potent catalysts for development,

The Art of Emotional Alchemy: Turning Negative Feelings into Positive Energy

healing, and transformation by taking steps to cultivate self-compassion and practise emotional alchemy.

*

The Art of Emotional Alchemy: Turning Negative Feelings into Positive Energy

The Mirror's Reflection: Facing Your Emotions Head-On

Although emotions are frequently viewed as something to be avoided or hidden, they are actually a vital aspect of being human. Emotions can lead us to a more fulfilling life and reveal important information about our inner world. Unfortunately, a lot of us have developed the ability to suppress or deny our emotions, which has caused a detachment from our own selves. The only real method to comprehend and change our emotions is to confront them head-on.

A potent metaphor for this procedure is the mirror. Our emotions can serve as a mirror for our inner reality, just as a physical mirror reflects our outside look. Looking in the mirror allows us to glimpse our true selves, warts and all. Similar to this, when we face our emotions, we can learn more about our innermost aspirations, anxieties, and beliefs.

The Art of Emotional Alchemy: Turning Negative Feelings into Positive Energy

Although it may be difficult and uncomfortable, this is crucial for emotional alchemy and personal development.

Developing self-awareness is a crucial component in dealing with our emotions. This calls for focusing on our inner experience and developing an interest in how we are experiencing. Allowing ourselves to feel whatever comes without attempting to alter or correct it might be beneficial when approaching our emotions with an attitude of compassion and non-judgment. We can begin to understand the underlying reasons and patterns of our emotions by recognising and accepting them.

Accepting responsibility for our emotions is a crucial component of facing our emotions. Although it can be tempting to put the responsibility for our emotional condition on other people or situations, we are ultimately in charge of how we feel. Although accepting this reality can be challenging, it is inspiring to know that we have

The Art of Emotional Alchemy: Turning Negative Feelings into Positive Energy

the power to change how we feel. By gaining control of our feelings, we may begin to consciously decide how we want to feel and react to events.

Journaling is a potent tool for overcoming our emotions. We can acquire perspective and clarity on our inner world by putting our thoughts and feelings down on paper. We might use journaling questions like "What am I feeling right now and why?" or "What is this emotion attempting to tell me?" to explore certain feelings or circumstances. By keeping a daily journal, we can begin to recognise themes and patterns in our emotional experience, which can lead us to greater self-awareness and development.

It's crucial to ask for help when dealing with your emotions. A therapist, support group, or close friend can serve as this. Expressing our feelings with others might make us feel less isolated and open our eyes to new

The Art of Emotional Alchemy: Turning Negative Feelings into Positive Energy

possibilities. It may also instil a sense of responsibility and drive to carry on with emotional alchemy.

In many facets of life, embracing our emotions is demonstrated. For instance, a person who experiences social anxiety can decide to go to a gathering despite feeling uneasy in order to face their fear and discover that it is not as terrifying as they had imagined. Or, someone who has gone through a traumatic situation could decide to go to therapy to work through their feelings and start to recover. These decisions need to be made with openness and courage, but the results can be tremendous personal change.

We are essentially facing ourselves when we confront our emotions. We are recognising that being human is messy, intricate, and lovely. We can achieve more wholeness and inner serenity by accepting all of who we are.

The Art of Emotional Alchemy: Turning Negative Feelings into Positive Energy

Looking in the mirror and asking oneself, "What am I avoiding? " is another method to use it as a tool for emotional alchemy. This query may bring to the surface feelings or circumstances that we are attempting to deny or brush off. We can begin the process of change and progress by recognising and facing these emotions.

Similar to this, we can use the mirror to work on our self-love and compassion. Our subconscious mind receives a strong signal that we are deserving of love and respect when we look at ourselves in the mirror with kindness and acceptance. We may feel better about ourselves and have less negative self-talk as a result.

It might be challenging to confront our feelings, so it's critical to keep in mind that it's acceptable to ask for support and assistance. According to Brené Brown's well-known adage, "Vulnerability is not weakness; it's our greatest measure of courage."

The Art of Emotional Alchemy: Turning Negative Feelings into Positive Energy

The benefits of emotional alchemy are worth the courage it takes to face our emotions and vulnerabilities.

The mirror can be a potent tool for emotional alchemy, to conclude. We can start to change the unfavourable patterns and ideas that hold us back by using it to reflect on our emotions and identify them. Practicing self-compassion and self-love in front of a mirror can also help us feel more confident and have less negative self-talk. Keep in mind that emotional alchemy is a journey, and it is acceptable to ask for assistance and support when needed.

*

The Art of Emotional Alchemy: Turning Negative Feelings into Positive Energy

The Alchemist's Forge: Crafting Your Emotional Future

We have the potential to create our own emotional future, just like an alchemist creates their own elixirs and potions. We have the ability to mould and mould our emotions as we choose because they are not predetermined. We will look at how to apply the techniques and ideas of emotional alchemy to forge the emotional future we desire in this chapter.

The Influence of Intentions

Setting intentions is one of the key strategies for influencing your emotional destiny. The blueprints for your emotional future, intentions provide you a defined direction to work in and an objective to aim for. While making plans, it's crucial to concentrate more on what you want to do than what you want to avoid.

The Art of Emotional Alchemy: Turning Negative Feelings into Positive Energy

You can direct your energy in a constructive direction and work towards a desired result in this way.

Energy flows where attention goes, according to the proverb. You may attract the energy and resources needed to make your goals happen by focusing your attention on them by setting clear intentions.

Self-Awareness: Its Significance

A strong sense of self-awareness is also necessary while shaping your emotional future. This entails being able to identify and comprehend your own feelings, triggers, and behavioural patterns. It is challenging to know where to focus your efforts and what adjustments to make in order to achieve your desired emotional state without self-awareness.

By engaging in activities like mindfulness, journaling, or counselling, one might develop self-awareness. You can

The Art of Emotional Alchemy: Turning Negative Feelings into Positive Energy

start to comprehend what triggers your emotions and what steps you can take to change them by becoming more conscious of them.

The Alchemist's Tools

You need to have a variety of tools at your disposal in order to shape your emotional future. These techniques include self-care, gratitude, visualisation, and meditation. Each of these instruments has a certain function and can assist you in changing unfavourable feelings into favourable ones.

For instance, meditation is an effective method for developing tranquillity and inner peace. You may educate your mind to be more resistant to stress and bad emotions by frequently practising meditation.

Another effective technique for influencing your emotional future is visualisation. You are effectively

The Art of Emotional Alchemy: Turning Negative Feelings into Positive Energy

drawing a road map for your mind to follow when you see yourself in a happy emotional state. This might assist you in attracting the energies and assets required to reach the desired emotional state.

Another crucial instrument for emotional alchemy is gratitude. You can change your emphasis from negative feelings to positive emotions by paying attention to the blessings in your life. It has been demonstrated that feeling grateful increases resilience to stress and general well-being.

In order to shape your emotional future, self-care is equally essential. You can feel more empowered and in control of your emotions by taking care of your physical, emotional, and mental needs. Exercise, a balanced diet, and spending time doing activities you enjoy are a few examples of this.

The Art of Emotional Alchemy: Turning Negative Feelings into Positive Energy

Let's use the case of someone who wishes to get rid of their anxiety and create a future filled with less stress. This person might begin by deciding to be at ease and at peace in their daily activities. So that they might become more conscious of their thoughts and feelings, they might then practise mindfulness meditation. They could also practise gratitude and visualisation to keep their thoughts on the good things in their lives. They might also prioritise things like exercise and time spent in nature as a kind of self-care.

Someone who desires to generate greater joy and happiness in their life is another example. This person might have made it a goal to feel joyful and content. Thus, by concentrating on the positive aspects of their lives, they can practise thankfulness. They might also employ visualisation to picture happy and contented events in their own lives.

The Art of Emotional Alchemy: Turning Negative Feelings into Positive Energy

The process of transformation will become simpler and more natural as you practise working with your emotions and honing your alchemical abilities. You will improve your ability to spot the trends and causes that lead to unfavourable feelings and your capacity to swiftly transform those emotions into favourable ones.

Emotional alchemy's ultimate objective is to change negative emotions into positive ones and use them as a source of energy for personal progress rather than to completely eradicate them. Paracelsus, a famous alchemist, reportedly stated, "Because nothing is without poisonous properties, everything is poisoned. Only the dose can make something poisonous."

In other words, negative emotions aren't always bad; it's just how we interact with them that might be harmful. We may harness the power of negative emotions and use them as a catalyst for development and change by learning to transform them into positive ones.

The Art of Emotional Alchemy: Turning Negative Feelings into Positive Energy

Remember Rumi's wise words as you proceed on your path as an emotional alchemist: "The wound is the place where the light enters you." Accept all of your feelings, even the bad ones, and use them to learn more about yourself and the world. You can turn any emotional sorrow into personal progress and enlightenment if you have the correct tools and mindset.

*

The Art of Emotional Alchemy: Turning Negative Feelings into Positive Energy

The Alchemy of Joy: Finding Happiness through Emotional Alchemy

A universal human urge is to pursue happiness. Everybody wants to be happy and pleased with their lives, but occasionally our negative emotions might get in the way. Emotional alchemy can help in this situation. We can build a route to genuine happiness by transforming negative emotions into positive ones.

The voyage of the alchemy of joy calls for focus, commitment, and repetition. Instead of repressing or ignoring our feelings, it entails learning to embrace and transform them. By doing this, we can develop an inner joy and peace that is independent of the outside world.

Gratitude is one of the keys to using emotional alchemy to find joy. A strong emotion like gratitude might help us change our perspective from what we lack to what we do have.

The Art of Emotional Alchemy: Turning Negative Feelings into Positive Energy

The ability to recognise the beauty in our surroundings and value life's basic joys comes from practising thankfulness. Gratitude is not only the greatest virtue, but also the parent of all the others, as the wise philosopher Cicero once observed.

Building wholesome relationships is a crucial component of the alchemy of joy. Our mental wellbeing can be greatly influenced by the people we choose to be in our lives; individuals who make us happy and support us while we face difficulties in life. "Surround yourself with those who lift you higher," the saying goes.

It's crucial to take part in things that make us happy and fulfilled. Finding meaning in our life can assist us in connecting with a sense of inner joy and purpose, whether it is by engaging in a pastime, spending time in nature, or working for a cause we care about.

The Art of Emotional Alchemy: Turning Negative Feelings into Positive Energy

Of course, finding happiness is not always simple. There will be times when we encounter unpleasant feelings, disappointments, and difficulties. But we may turn those experiences into chances for development and self-discovery by accepting our feelings and employing the techniques of emotional alchemy.

The secret to life, according to the alchemist Paulo Coelho, is to fall seven times and get back up eight times. We can learn to use emotional alchemy to change our suffering into insight, our failures into learning opportunities, and our sorrow into purpose.

Understanding that happiness is a state of mind is one of the most crucial elements of discovering joy through emotional alchemy. It's not something that can be obtained by relying on outside factors or material goods. Instead, it originates internally, from how we decide to interpret and react to the environment around us.

The Art of Emotional Alchemy: Turning Negative Feelings into Positive Energy

When it comes to this, emotional alchemy is useful. We can change our viewpoint and cultivate a more optimistic outlook on life by transforming negative emotions into good ones. Let's say, for illustration, that you face some criticism at work. You could decide to view it as an opportunity to learn and grow, to hone your talents and get better at what you do rather than feeling irritated or furious. You can feel better by turning a bad experience into a good one by changing the way you think about it.

This is obviously easier said than done. To alter our thoughts and responses to the outside environment, it needs work and practise. The good news is that emotional alchemy gives us the means to accomplish this. We can progressively change our perspective and build a more optimistic outlook on life by employing practices like mindfulness, self-reflection, and thankfulness.

The Art of Emotional Alchemy: Turning Negative Feelings into Positive Energy

Let's take the scenario when you are anxious and overloaded at work. By taking a few minutes to concentrate on your breathing and bring yourself into the present moment, you can try practising mindfulness. Your mind will become more at ease, and your anxiety levels will decrease. As an alternative, consider making a list of your blessings in order to keep your mind on the wonderful things in your life and to remind yourself of all the reasons to be grateful.

With practice, these methods can assist you in cultivating a happier and more fulfilled view on life. Naturally, this is only one illustration of the many methods and approaches that can be employed to nurture joy and happiness through emotional alchemy.

Consider a person who experiences anxiety and depression as an example. They discover that they are unable to find delight in anything and are feeling overpowered and despairing. They find ways to

The Art of Emotional Alchemy: Turning Negative Feelings into Positive Energy

transform bad emotions into positive ones, though, and start to change their perspective as a result of engaging in emotional alchemy. They begin to practise mindfulness and gratitude, concentrating on the positive aspects of their lives and making baby strides towards personal development. They gradually start to experience more optimism and hope, delight in everyday pleasures, and feel more content all around. They have changed their perspective on life and discovered the happiness they were looking for thanks to emotional alchemy.

To sum up, emotional alchemy is a potent instrument for discovering fulfilment and happiness in life. We can change our viewpoint and cultivate a more optimistic outlook on life by transforming negative emotions into good ones. We may progressively create a more positive mindset and discover delight in every moment by employing techniques like mindfulness, self-reflection, and gratitude, but this requires time and work.

The Art of Emotional Alchemy: Turning Negative Feelings into Positive Energy

The Alchemist's Elixir: Cultivating Emotional Wellness

A crucial component of general wellbeing is emotional wellness. We are better equipped to handle life's obstacles, uphold strong relationships, and enjoy more joy and fulfilment in our daily lives when we feel emotionally balanced. But getting emotional wellbeing is not always simple. It calls for effort, endurance, and a readiness to accept and process uncomfortable feelings. The practice of emotional alchemy as a method for fostering emotional wellbeing will be discussed in this chapter.

The Art of Emotional Alchemy

Emotional alchemy allows us to change bad emotions into positive ones, much as alchemists may change base metals into gold. Understanding that our emotions are pliable and changeable rather than permanent is the key

The Art of Emotional Alchemy: Turning Negative Feelings into Positive Energy

to developing emotional wellness. We may change bad emotions into positive ones with the correct tools and methods, such as changing fear into bravery or sadness into appreciation.

We must first become conscious of our emotions in order to practise emotional alchemy and create emotional wellbeing. This entails pausing to consider our feelings and developing greater sensitivity to the emotions that surface within us during the day. Understanding our emotions will help us start to spot patterns and triggers that lead to unfavourable feelings.

After we become emotionally aware, we may begin to use the principles of emotional alchemy to change bad feelings into positive ones. To do this, we can use techniques like mindfulness, meditation, and positive affirmations to rewire our thoughts and emotions.

The Art of Emotional Alchemy: Turning Negative Feelings into Positive Energy

It also entails learning constructive coping skills like exercise, creative expression, or talking to a dependable friend or counsellor.

Infusion of the Alchemist

In order to perform emotional alchemy and nurture emotional wellbeing, we must mix a potent concoction of methods, routines, and practises that promote emotional health. Although some of these ingredients have already been mentioned in prior chapters, solidification of such concepts must be ingrained and utilised to create a potent elixir in the alchemy of emotion. A personal elixir should contain the following essential components:

Gratitude is a strong feeling that can help us turn our attention from negative to good thoughts. Focusing on the things in our lives for which we are grateful, whether it's a romantic relationship, a breathtaking sunset, or a

The Art of Emotional Alchemy: Turning Negative Feelings into Positive Energy

straightforward act of kindness, is part of the practice of cultivating gratitude.

Self-talk that is constructive, can be thought of as the process in which we talk to ourselves from the inside, and has a big impact on how we feel and how we're doing. We can transform unfavourable ideas and beliefs into good ones by developing a positive self-talk routine. In order to do this, we must deliberately concentrate on our abilities, successes, and good traits while utilising affirmations to support these views.

Expressing oneself creatively can be a potent approach to let go of bad emotions and foster positive ones. Examples of creative endeavours include writing, music, and painting. In addition to helping us access a sense of flow and awareness, creative expression enables us to communicate our emotions in a healthy and safe way.

The Art of Emotional Alchemy: Turning Negative Feelings into Positive Energy

Bringing our attention to the present moment while being judgement-free is mindfulness. We can lessen worries about the future or regrets about the past by keeping our attention in the now. Meditation, deep breathing exercises, or simply taking a few minutes each day to tune into our senses and notice our surroundings are all examples of mindfulness activities.

Together with mindfulness, adding regular exercise to your schedule might help you feel better emotionally. Exercise is a good way to relieve stress and negative emotions because it releases endorphins, which are natural mood enhancers.

Also, it's critical to give your body healthful meals to eat and to emphasise getting enough sleep. Your total mental and physical wellness can be supported by a balanced diet and enough sleep.

The Art of Emotional Alchemy: Turning Negative Feelings into Positive Energy

It's important to keep in mind that developing emotional wellness is a continuous process that calls for continued work and attention. You may lay a strong foundation for long-lasting emotional well-being by frequently practising emotional alchemy and implementing these tools into your life.

Our emotional health can be significantly impacted by forming good habits like regular exercise, adequate sleep, and a balanced diet. We are better able to handle stress and feel good emotions when we take care of our physical health.

Michael Phelps, who won the gold medal at the Olympics, is one example of a person who has developed emotional wholeness. Despite his impressive athletic record, Phelps has also been open about his melancholy and anxiety issues. He uses a number of techniques, such as regular therapy sessions, regular exercise, and mindfulness meditation, to preserve his

The Art of Emotional Alchemy: Turning Negative Feelings into Positive Energy

emotional well-being. Phelps has found success in his sport as well as long-lasting happiness and fulfilment in his personal life by putting his emotional well-being first.

Finally, emotional alchemy is a transformational technique that enables us to change unfavourable emotions into favourable ones and foster emotional wellness. Self-awareness, intention, and the appropriate tools are necessary for this lifelong journey in order to promote the transition.

We have discovered the magic within us, transformed pain into purpose, mixed emotions with intention, emerged from the ashes of negative emotions, woven positivity throughout our lives, ignited transformation, faced our emotions head-on, and created our emotional future through the practises and techniques described in this book.

The Art of Emotional Alchemy: Turning Negative Feelings into Positive Energy

We can build emotional wellbeing and experience happiness and fulfilment in our lives by accepting the alchemical process and engaging our emotions with inquiry, compassion, and a readiness to change.

According to Paracelsus, a philosopher and alchemist, "Just transforming one form into another is the essence of alchemy. Lead becomes gold thanks to alchemy. The emotional alchemist changes unfavourable feelings into advantageous ones."

Let's all work to become emotional alchemists and transform our rotten emotions into the life-giving elixir of gold.

*

The Art of Emotional Alchemy: Turning Negative Feelings into Positive Energy

The Alchemist's Wisdom: Insights for Navigating Your Emotions

You have gained useful skills and knowledge for transforming unfavourable feelings, nurturing optimism, and planning your emotional future via your emotional alchemy trip. But just like on any voyage, there may be instances when you run into unforeseen difficulties.

In this chapter, we'll look at the knowledge that can help you get through those difficult times and offer you guidance for navigating the ups and downs of your emotional terrain.

The first realisation is that emotions are just what they are—neither good nor harmful. They can feel either positively or negatively depending on how we choose to interpret them. As a result, it's crucial to approach each feeling with curiosity and an open mind rather than with opposition or judgement.

The Art of Emotional Alchemy: Turning Negative Feelings into Positive Energy

The second realisation is that emotions serve as messengers, informing us about both our inner selves and the outside world. We can better understand ourselves and our needs when we learn to hear these messages without passing judgement.

The third realisation is that emotions are interrelated and that one emotion can set off a cascade of others. Instead of merely responding to the feeling at the surface level, we can address the underlying problem by determining the cause of our emotions.

The fourth realisation is that emotions are a normal aspect of human experience and that it is acceptable to experience them. We don't need to hide or repress our feelings because doing so can result in emotional repression and jeopardise both our mental and physical wellbeing.

The Art of Emotional Alchemy: Turning Negative Feelings into Positive Energy

The fifth insight is that mindfulness, self-awareness, and deliberate action can change how we feel. We can turn negative emotions into constructive ones and use them as fuel for our development and change by engaging in emotional alchemy.

Have an open mind, be interested, and be kind to yourself as you navigate your emotional environment. When you experience difficult emotions, consider what they are attempting to tell you and what you can do to address the underlying problem.

For instance, instead of merely attempting to get through feelings of stress and anxiety at work, take a step back and investigate the underlying reason for your feelings. Is it a demanding boss, a challenging coworker, or something else? You may make your working environment more enduring and fulfilling by dealing with the root cause.

The Art of Emotional Alchemy: Turning Negative Feelings into Positive Energy

It can be beneficial to practise mindfulness techniques such as deep breathing, meditation, or grounding exercises when experiencing strong emotions. You can lessen the intensity of your emotions and maintain your present-moment awareness with the aid of these techniques.

Finally, keep in mind that feelings are transient. You can get more adept at navigating them because they are dynamic and ever-changing with practice.

Lao Tzu, a philosopher, famously remarked, "Strength is in controlling others. The actual source of power lies inside." You can achieve control over your emotions and use them as a catalyst for development and transformation by practising self-awareness, mindfulness, and emotional alchemy.

The Art of Emotional Alchemy: Turning Negative Feelings into Positive Energy

Ultimately, managing our emotions may be both a difficult and rewarding task. We can design a more contented and meaningful existence by accepting the wisdom of emotional alchemy and remaining open to the insights that our emotions offer. Keep in mind to be present in the moment, practise taking conscious action in the direction of your goals, and approach your emotions with enquiry and compassion. You can navigate any emotional environment that comes your way if you have these skills in your toolkit.

*

The Art of Emotional Alchemy: Turning Negative Feelings into Positive Energy

The Art of Inner Alchemy: Transforming Your Inner Landscape

The process of altering one's inner landscape is known as inner alchemy. Through the process of inner alchemy, we may also change our bad emotions into positive ones, just as an alchemist can change base metals into gold. This chapter will examine the various facets of inner alchemy and how we might make use of this age-old knowledge to improve our lives.

The idea that everything is related is one of the foundational ideas of inner alchemy. Our ideas, feelings, and deeds are all intertwined, and by changing one, we can cause a chain reaction that alters every aspect of who we are. The Chinese notion of Yin and Yang, which stand for the harmony and balance of opposing forces, serves as an illustration of this interconnection. We can attain equilibrium and harmony within ourselves by utilising the energies of Yin and Yang.

The Art of Emotional Alchemy: Turning Negative Feelings into Positive Energy

The practice of mindfulness is another element of inner alchemy. Being mindful means paying attention to the present and immersing oneself in the experience. We may observe our thoughts and feelings objectively and learn more about ourselves by being conscious of them. By this exercise, we may spot destructive thinking and behaviour patterns and replace them with constructive ones.

The development of interior virtues like compassion, gratitude, and forgiveness is another aspect of inner alchemy. These qualities can aid us in cultivating a more optimistic attitude on life and are the cornerstones of emotional wellness. We can cultivate a sense of inner tranquillity and harmony that permeates every aspect of our daily life by practising these virtues.

The instruments of inner alchemy in the alchemist's workshop include self-reflection, journaling, and meditation.

The Art of Emotional Alchemy: Turning Negative Feelings into Positive Energy

With the help of these techniques, we can explore our deeper selves and gain understanding of our emotions and thinking processes. We can start to change our inner landscape and bring about positive change in our lives if we routinely engage in these techniques.

Patience is a virtue that is essential for inner alchemy to succeed. We must be patient in order to change our negative emotions into positive ones, much as an alchemist must be while transforming base metals into gold. Change doesn't happen overnight, but with perseverance and commitment, we can bring about long-lasting change.

"Nature does not hurry, yet everything is completed," said Lao Tzu. The process of inner alchemy develops naturally and at its own pace. We can nurture emotional wellbeing and change our internal environment by having faith in this process and staying dedicated to our practice.

The Art of Emotional Alchemy: Turning Negative Feelings into Positive Energy

The act of loving-kindness meditation is one instance of inner alchemy in action. Sending loving and compassionate thoughts to ourselves and other people is a part of this practice. We can make a good impact on the lives of others around us by fostering a sense of love and compassion within ourselves.

The habit of keeping a gratitude journal is another illustration. We can turn our attention away from negativity and build a more upbeat mindset by dwelling on the blessings in our life. This routine can enable us to view the world with an abundance- and gratitude-focused perspective.

Finally, the practice of inner alchemy is a potent means of reshaping our emotional landscape. We can bring about long-lasting beneficial change in our lives by utilising the power of mindfulness, developing our inner values, and regularly reflecting on our actions.

The Art of Emotional Alchemy: Turning Negative Feelings into Positive Energy

Let us keep Rumi's words in mind as we embark on this road of personal transformation "Yesterday I was clever, so I wanted to change the world. Today I am wise, so I am changing myself."

*

The Art of Emotional Alchemy: Turning Negative Feelings into Positive Energy

The Alchemist's Compass: Navigating the Terrain of Your Emotions

It might be difficult to navigate our emotional landscape. Our emotions can be erratic and ever-shifting, like a raging ocean. But much like a sailor uses a compass to explore the open ocean, we may utilise the instruments of emotional alchemy to help us navigate the complicated terrain of our emotions.

Understanding that emotions are a natural part of our human experience rather than something to be conquered or overcome is the first step in learning to manage them. We must acknowledge that feelings are simply a mirror of our interior condition and are neither good nor negative.

Once we acknowledge that our emotions are real, we may start using the tools of emotional alchemy to help us. The practice of mindfulness, which is being fully

The Art of Emotional Alchemy: Turning Negative Feelings into Positive Energy

present in the moment and noticing our feelings without passing judgement, is a crucial skill. This kind of emotional observation can help us better comprehend our emotions and increase our emotional intelligence.

The practice of self-reflection is another weapon in our toolkit for emotional alchemy. We can recognise patterns in our emotional reactions and get more understanding of our mental processes by taking the time to reflect on our feelings. We can also start to recognise the underlying values and beliefs that shape our emotions through self-reflection.

It's crucial to keep in mind that our emotions are not separate from the outside world. Our interactions with others, our media consumption, and the events in our own life all have an impact on them. We can start to traverse our emotional landscape with greater clarity if we become more conscious of these outside stimuli and how they affect our feelings.

The Art of Emotional Alchemy: Turning Negative Feelings into Positive Energy

Furthermore, keep in mind that emotional alchemy is a continuous process. Growing and learning about oneself is a continuous process. We must constantly alter our emotional compass to take into account the constantly shifting terrain of our emotions, much as a sailor must do to account for shifting winds and currents.

Picture yourself as a recent college graduate with a new job. You are thrilled about the opportunity, but you are also apprehensive about how you will manage the workload and fit in with the team. You observe as your first week on the job gets under way that your coworkers are not as amiable as you had hoped, and your supervisor looks distant and unapproachable. You start to feel overburdened, defeated, and you start to question your skills.

It's critical in this scenario to navigate your feelings and responses to the situation using your alchemist's compass. Taking a step back and doing an unbiased

The Art of Emotional Alchemy: Turning Negative Feelings into Positive Energy

analysis of the circumstance is one approach to achieve this. You could ponder things like:

1. What is the situation's reality?
2. Am I forming assumptions or leaping to conclusions?
3. Are there any chances I can take advantage of or sources I can use to help me succeed?

You can obtain a clearer perspective and make better decisions about how to proceed by adopting a more logical and balanced approach. You can try to comprehend your boss's and your coworkers' viewpoints and motivations by using your emotional intelligence to empathise with them. By doing so, you may be able to forge better bonds with others and foster a more encouraging and positive work atmosphere.

While dealing with challenging emotions, it's also critical to have a strong sense of self-awareness and

The Art of Emotional Alchemy: Turning Negative Feelings into Positive Energy

self-regulation. This is being open and honest with yourself about your feelings and taking action to control them in a positive and healthy way. For instance, you might engage in mindfulness or meditation to relax your body and mind, or you might consult with a dependable friend or mentor to get advice and support.

In conclusion, the landscape of our emotions might be difficult to travel across, but with the aid of emotional alchemy, we can find our way through even the most difficult situations. Seneca, a philosopher, famously observed, "We don't have a limited lifespan; rather, we waste a lot of it. If it were all well invested, life is long enough and a suitably ample quantity has been given to us for the finest accomplishments." We can live more fulfilled and meaningful lives by making an investment in our emotional health and learning to negotiate the challenging terrain of our emotions.

*

The Art of Emotional Alchemy: Turning Negative Feelings into Positive Energy

The Alchemist's Journey: A Path of Transformation

The process of emotional alchemy is a journey, much like the journey of life. The voyage of emotional alchemy requires a path to follow, just as every journey requires a map or compass. It's a voyage of personal development, expansion, and transformation. We learn to accept the strength of our emotions and use them as a tool for personal growth and development as we make our way through the ups and downs of life.

The road to emotional alchemy is not always straightforward, just like any journey. There will be times of doubt, discomfort, and possibly even pain. But it is via these difficulties that we must develop and learn. The path of emotional alchemy demands bravery, openness, and a readiness to confront our fears and limits. As we go out on this path, we come to trust both the transformational process and ourselves.

The Art of Emotional Alchemy: Turning Negative Feelings into Positive Energy

It's necessary to have a specific target in mind before beginning any journey. The goal of emotional alchemy is a state of being rather than a geographical location. It is the condition of inner tranquillity, emotional fortitude, and genuine self-expression. This is a state that can only be attained by accepting the whole range of our emotions and using them as sources of power, insight, and personal development.

We come across a number of instruments, methods, and practises that guide us across the landscape of our emotions as we travel the path of emotional alchemy. These techniques include thankfulness, self-reflection, self-compassion, and many others. These exercises support the growth of a strong sense of self and the capacity to handle our emotions with intelligence and expertise.

The Art of Emotional Alchemy: Turning Negative Feelings into Positive Energy

Emotional alchemy's journey is rarely a straight one. It is a continuous process that calls for commitment, perseverance, and dedication. We must be willing to let go of outdated routines and ideas in favour of embracing change. We must develop a strong sense of self-love and self-compassion and learn to embrace ourselves completely, with all of our faults and defects.

Emotional alchemy's journey is ultimately one of transformation. It's a path towards improving ourselves and leading a life filled with meaning, joy, and contentment. As we set out on this path, we develop the ability to alchemize our own emotions, turning suffering into knowledge, fear into bravery, and darkness into light.

"The alchemist is the person who transforms everything into love." - Paulo Coelho

The Art of Emotional Alchemy: Turning Negative Feelings into Positive Energy

Think of a person who has endured years of anguish. Nothing seemed to be working despite their attempts at counselling, medication, and different self-help methods. The idea of emotional alchemy is then introduced to them, and they decide to test it. By using the transmutation and integration processes, they start to become aware of their worried thoughts and feelings. They gradually but surely begin to notice a change in their emotions. People can better regulate their anxiety because they feel more in control of it. They start to experience personal growth and transformation as they continue to practice emotional alchemy.

"The journey of a thousand miles begins with one step."
- Lao Tzu

In conclusion, although the route of emotional alchemy is a path of transformation that results in better emotional wellbeing and inner serenity, it is not an easy one. It is a process of self-discovery and self-mastery

The Art of Emotional Alchemy: Turning Negative Feelings into Positive Energy

where we learn to successfully negotiate the emotional landscape. With the power of our own inner alchemy, we can change our negative emotions into positive ones just as the alchemist converts base metals into gold. The trip is one that calls for endurance, perseverance, and a readiness to confront our inner demons, but the benefits are great. We can design a life that is characterised by love, joy, and inner peace through emotional alchemy.

"Change the way you look at things and the things you look at change." - Wayne Dyer

*

The Art of Emotional Alchemy: Turning Negative Feelings into Positive Energy

The Alchemy of Forgiveness: Healing Your Emotional Wounds

An important part of emotional alchemy is forgiveness. It can be very detrimental to our mental health and wellbeing to hold onto anger, resentment, and grudges. Although it can be difficult, forgiving people who have harmed us and letting go of our pain is essential for our own healing and development.

Forgiveness is the process of changing bad emotions into positive ones, just as alchemists transmute base metals into gold. When we forgive, we set ourselves free from the bonds of unfavourable feelings and enable ourselves to proceed with a fresh sense of freedom and optimism.

It's not about rationalising someone else's actions or downplaying the harm they caused us in order to forgive them. It's about making the decision to discover inner peace and let go of our bitterness and hate towards them.

The Art of Emotional Alchemy: Turning Negative Feelings into Positive Energy

We give ourselves the opportunity to experience new things by forgiving people who have wronged us.

Yet it's not always simple to forgive. When the wounds are severe, the path can be lengthy and challenging. It's crucial to keep in mind that forgiving someone is a process that requires time, patience, and practise rather than being a one-time event. While it's acceptable to feel wounded and enraged, we must also be prepared to move past these feelings in order to forgive.

Consider things from the other person's viewpoint as a way to practise forgiveness. While it does not obligate us to support their acts, it might provide us insight into their motivations. By doing this, we can develop compassion and empathy for the one who injured us, which may make it simpler for us to pardon them.

The Art of Emotional Alchemy: Turning Negative Feelings into Positive Energy

Meditation that emphasises mindfulness is another method for forgiving. We can develop a sense of inner peace and compassion for ourselves and other people by keeping our attention on the here and now and monitoring our thoughts and emotions without passing judgement. We can develop forgiveness and learn to let go of unpleasant feelings by practising mindfulness.

"Forgiveness is not only an occasional deed; it is a permanent attitude," Desmond Tutu once said. It takes a lifetime of practise to be able to let go of our hurt and choose love and compassion above it. By practising forgiveness, we can use our emotional scars as a source of resiliency and strength.

For illustration purposes, Sarah had harboured animosity towards her ex-husband for several years following their divorce. She was saddened and enraged by how he had treated her and their kids throughout the procedure.

The Art of Emotional Alchemy: Turning Negative Feelings into Positive Energy

She eventually saw, however, that hanging onto her rage was preventing her from moving on with her life and just doing herself harm.

Sarah was able to let go of her bitterness towards her ex-husband by attending therapy sessions and putting forgiveness into practice. She made the decision to consider things from his point of view and comprehend the reasons behind his actions. She was able to find calm inside herself and let out her rage by doing this.

Forgiveness for Sarah was a process that required time and repetition rather than occurring all at once. But she felt lighter and more liberated with each step she took in the direction of forgiveness. She came to understand that forgiving her ex-husband meant choosing to let go of her rage and achieve inner peace rather than justifying his actions.

The Art of Emotional Alchemy: Turning Negative Feelings into Positive Energy

It's critical to keep in mind that forgiving someone is a process, not a one-time thing. To heal mental scars and let go of the anguish requires dedication, patience, and effort. But with the alchemist's perspective and the practice of emotional alchemy, forgiving may be a transforming process that results in healing, growth, and peace.

According to Maya Angelou, "Forgiveness is one of the best gifts you can give to yourself. Pardon everyone." One of the most effective means of emotional growth and healing is forgiveness. We create room for love, compassion, and joy to enter our lives by letting go of the grief and pain.

In conclusion, although the trip towards emotional alchemy is difficult, it is also valuable. We can develop self-awareness and compassion, change bad emotions into positive ones, and achieve healing and progress via the practice of emotional alchemy.

The Art of Emotional Alchemy: Turning Negative Feelings into Positive Energy

An important part of emotional alchemy is forgiveness. It enables us to free ourselves from the bonds of unfavourable feelings and proceed with a fresh sense of freedom and optimism. We can let go of our suffering and opt for love and compassion by learning to forgive.

*

The Art of Emotional Alchemy: Turning Negative Feelings into Positive Energy

The Alchemy of Gratitude: Cultivating a Positive Mindset

Gratitude is one of the most transformational and potent weapons we can employ on the path of emotional alchemy. A grateful mindset enables us to keep our attention on the positive parts of our lives rather than on the drawbacks. It has the ability to alter our viewpoint, our emotions, and our general wellbeing. As we practise thankfulness, we become more capable of overcoming obstacles in life and are more likely to feel joy and contentment.

Even the most difficult circumstances can be improved by being grateful. It has the capacity to mend our wounds, deepen our relationships with others, and enable us to perceive the goodness and beauty in the world. By practising thankfulness, we can change our bad thoughts and feelings into positive ones, much as an alchemist can change base metals into gold.

The Art of Emotional Alchemy: Turning Negative Feelings into Positive Energy

There are many advantages to being grateful. According to studies, people who routinely express appreciation are less likely to experience melancholy and anxiety, have better relationships, sleep better, and even have better physical health. By emphasising what we have rather than what we need, gratitude enables us to enjoy the present moment and cultivate a more upbeat view on life.

A straightforward but effective practice that we may adopt into our daily lives is practising thankfulness. We might begin by simply setting aside some time each day to think about the things we have to be thankful for. It might be something insignificant like the warmth of a cup of tea or the sun shining, or it might be something more important like a love relationship or a rewarding career. We are more likely to notice and value the good things in our lives if we concentrate on these things and express our gratitude for them.

The Art of Emotional Alchemy: Turning Negative Feelings into Positive Energy

By keeping a thankfulness notebook, you may strengthen your gratitude in significant ways. We may teach our minds to concentrate on the good and create a more upbeat view by listing the things we are grateful for every day. In times of difficulty, it can also serve as a reminder of the positive aspects of our existence.

By deeds of kindness, you can grow gratitude in profound ways. In addition to improving the lives of those we help, when we do good deeds for others, we also feel delight and fulfilment in ourselves. This sensation of well-being might encourage us to practise thankfulness and increase our appreciation for the good things in our life.

Furthermore, it's critical to keep in mind that thankfulness is not limited to happy occasions. Seeing the positive in challenging circumstances and learning to value the lessons we may take away from them are also important aspects of this.

The Art of Emotional Alchemy: Turning Negative Feelings into Positive Energy

With a grateful attitude, we are more likely to overcome obstacles and learn from the experience.

"Gratitude makes meaning of our past, brings calm for today, and generates a vision for tomorrow," writes author Melody Beattie. Through practising appreciation, we can change our perspective, enhance our wellbeing, and deal with obstacles more calmly with resiliency.

When we give thanks, we turn our attention away from unpleasant feelings and onto the good things in our lives. This perspective change has the potential to significantly impact both our physical and mental wellbeing.

Like a garden, gratitude requires care and attention. We can cultivate it by consciously focusing on the wonderful things in our lives, expressing our appreciation to others, and routinely practising thankfulness exercises.

The Art of Emotional Alchemy: Turning Negative Feelings into Positive Energy

Being grateful involves more than just feeling good; it also involves doing good. We are more likely to be kind and empathetic towards others when we are appreciative, which can enhance our interpersonal connections and relationships.

According to writer Melody Beattie, "The fullness of life is unlocked through gratitude. It makes what we already have more than enough. Denial is transformed into acceptance, disorder into order, and obscurity into clarity. A meal may become a feast, a house can become a home, and a stranger can become a friend thanks to it."

An investigation that was presented in the Journal of Personality and Social Psychology provides an illustration of the effectiveness of thankfulness. According to the study, participants who engaged in gratitude practises for just three weeks were happier and had lower levels of depression than those who did not.

The Art of Emotional Alchemy: Turning Negative Feelings into Positive Energy

Even six months after the activities were finished, the benefits of thankfulness persisted.

In conclusion, developing a grateful mindset can significantly improve our emotional health and general quality of life. We may build a positive feedback loop that results in more happiness, better relationships, and better physical health by concentrating on the positive aspects of our lives and expressing our gratitude for them.

*

The Art of Emotional Alchemy: Turning Negative Feelings into Positive Energy

The Alchemy of Love: Transmuting Negative Emotions into Love

Love is a strong force that can change unfavourable feelings into favourable ones. The transformation of sorrow and anguish into joy and happiness is the purest kind of emotional alchemy. The alchemy of love includes self-love, love for others, and love for the environment in addition to romantic love. It involves making the decision to find the positive in every circumstance, especially when it seems hopeless and challenging.

When we are able to transform unfavourable feelings into love, we unleash a positive energy that can influence those around us. Love is contagious, and when we give it out, we receive it back. All the goodness of life is drawn in like a magnet by it.

The Art of Emotional Alchemy: Turning Negative Feelings into Positive Energy

The alchemy of love is not always simple, though. It calls on us to surrender our ego, to be open to vulnerability, and to believe in the strength of love. It entails choosing to see the best in people even when they may not deserve it, letting go of anger and resentment, and forgiving those who have wounded us.

Gratitude is one of the most effective practices for developing the alchemy of love. We can change our energy from negative to positive by concentrating on the things for which we are grateful. Gratitude allows us to experience the wealth of love that is all around us. When we feel thankful, we view the world through fresh eyes and experience a shift in reality. Everything starts to look more beautiful to us, and we start to feel more love.

"Love is the bridge between you and everything." - Rumi

The Art of Emotional Alchemy: Turning Negative Feelings into Positive Energy

Compassion is another technique to develop the chemistry of love. When we are compassionate towards others, we can look past their flaws and comprehend the hardship and grief they might be going through.
Our hearts become more open to love as a result of being able to relate to people on a deeper level. We can see the world from other people's perspectives and put ourselves in their shoes when we are compassionate.

"Love and compassion are necessities, not luxuries. Without them, humanity cannot survive." - Dalai Lama

The alchemy of love includes the importance of self-love. We may freely love others when we first love ourselves. We develop into a source of love and light that spreads optimism. Self-love entails accepting oneself as they are, flaws and all, and believing that they are all worthy of love and happiness.

"Love is not about possession. Love is about appreciation." - Osho

The Art of Emotional Alchemy: Turning Negative Feelings into Positive Energy

The alchemy of love is a lifetime quest that calls for endurance, perseverance, and commitment. It's about choosing appreciation over negativity, love over fear, and forgiveness over resentment. We become alchemists of the heart, affecting both our own lives and the lives of people around us, when we are able to change unloving emotions into love.

It's important to keep in mind that alchemy is a lifelong process, particularly in the area of emotions. To transform bad emotions into positive ones, one must pay close attention and put forth constant effort. The benefits, nevertheless, are enormous. Emotional alchemy is a technique that can help us live happier, more peaceful, and fulfilled lives.

The art of alchemy, according to the renowned philosopher and alchemist Paracelsus, is to transform base metals into gold.

The Art of Emotional Alchemy: Turning Negative Feelings into Positive Energy

We can use this technique to transform unfavourable feelings into the precious metals of love and joy in the world of emotions. It's a transformational process that calls for fortitude, tenacity, and the desire to examine and face our worst fears and traumas.

But, as we do the emotional alchemy, we can discover that the gold we were looking for was actually already inside of ourselves. As above, so below; as within, so without, declared the ancient alchemist Hermes Trismegistus. Our outer environment is a reflection of our inner world, and we may surround ourselves with a beautiful and abundant world by transforming our negative feelings into love and joy.

*

The Art of Emotional Alchemy: Turning Negative Feelings into Positive Energy

The Alchemy of Creativity: Harnessing Your Emotions for Creative Inspiration

Emotions are a potent source of creative inspiration. They provide our creativity with fuel and give our ideas life. Our ability to control our emotions opens up a whole new range of creative possibilities. This chapter will examine the relationship between emotions and creativity as well as how the two are intertwined.

Making something new or creative is only one aspect of creativity; another is using our emotions to change the environment around us. As we create, we give life to something that was before nonexistent. To make something new and beautiful, to express ourselves, and to connect with others, we use our emotions. We can access a source of inspiration that can fuel our creativity when we connect with our emotions.

The Art of Emotional Alchemy: Turning Negative Feelings into Positive Energy

Our emotions can be transformed into art, music, writing, or any other form of expression through the alchemy of creativity. It is about connecting with others and using our emotions to encourage us. When we create, we transform our feelings into something tangible that other people may experience and share with them.

"Creativity is the way I share my soul with the world." - Brene Brown

As emotions are the foundation of creativity, our work would be lifeless and void without them. Our feelings can be changed via creativity into something meaningful and productive. It allows us to more deeply connect with others by expressing our emotions with them.

We are enacting an emotional alchemy when we create. We are making something real and palpable, like a picture or a song, out of something intangible, like an

The Art of Emotional Alchemy: Turning Negative Feelings into Positive Energy

emotion. By doing this, we turn our feelings into something that other people can understand and relate to.

"To be creative means to be in love with life. You can be creative only if you love life enough that you want to enhance its beauty, you want to bring a little more music to it, a little more poetry to it, a little more dance to it." - Osho

A potent method of emotional healing is creativity. It enables us to take our suffering, misery, and anxieties and turn them into something lovely. We transform something negative into something positive when we create. Our emotions are being transformed into something that can make us and other people happy.

Scenario about Creativity

In her life, Emily is going through a challenging moment. After a recent split, she is currently dealing

The Art of Emotional Alchemy: Turning Negative Feelings into Positive Energy

with feelings of melancholy and loneliness. She makes the decision to let her emotions inspire her creativity because she has always loved to sketch.

She paints and draws for hours every day, finding inspiration from her feelings. She uses dark hues and robust brushstrokes to depict her feelings of sadness and pain in a series of paintings that represent her emotions.

She starts to experience a sense of release and relief as she keeps on creating. She finds that the act of channelling her feelings into something physical is therapeutic and that the act of creating allows her to do so in a healthy way.

The Art of Emotional Alchemy: Turning Negative Feelings into Positive Energy

Emily's artwork starts to change with time. Her use of bolder hues and lighter brushstrokes signal a renewed sense of optimism and hope. She starts to share her art with people as her work gets more upbeat and joyous.

Emily is able to change her unfavourable emotions into something lovely and uplifting through her paintings. Her artwork makes those who see it happy and joyful because she has a deeper ability to connect with people. For Emily, creativity has evolved into a type of emotional alchemy that enables her to traverse the chasm of pain and despair.

We can change our feelings into something lovely and meaningful by expressing them creatively.

Consider a period when you experienced intense feelings, such as joy, rage, grief, or another emotion. Did you notice a certain artistic outlet attracting your attention? Maybe you composed music, painted a

The Art of Emotional Alchemy: Turning Negative Feelings into Positive Energy

picture, or wrote a poem. When we do this, we transform our feelings into something that other people may appreciate and perhaps even be inspired by.

Additionally, the process of producing itself can be therapeutic. A well-known type of psychotherapy called art therapy encourages artistic expression as a means of healing and personal development. People can utilise many artistic mediums to explore and process their feelings in a secure and encouraging atmosphere by working with a skilled therapist.

When we embrace our creativity, we have access to a wealth of motivation and inner strength. We become into alchemists, changing our unprocessed feelings into something lovely and profound.

Picasso reportedly remarked that "art cleanses the grime of ordinary life from the psyche." As a result, the next time you feel like your emotions are taking over, try

The Art of Emotional Alchemy: Turning Negative Feelings into Positive Energy

picking up a paintbrush, a pen, or an instrument. See what magic you can conjure by letting your feelings guide your creative expression.

The process of changing our unprocessed emotions into something uplifting and affirming of life is known as emotional alchemy. It calls for fortitude, self-awareness, and the readiness to engage in the inner task. We may nurture emotional wellbeing, promote positivity, and alter our lives by applying the strategies and methods of emotional alchemy.

According to the great philosopher Aristotle, "Excellence is a habit rather than a one-time event. You become what you consistently do." Our potential can be unlocked and we can live our best lives by developing the habit of emotional alchemy. So let's all learn how to alchemize our emotions and become the finest versions of ourselves.

The Art of Emotional Alchemy: Turning Negative Feelings into Positive Energy

The Alchemy of Connection: Building Positive Relationships

Because we are social beings, relationships are fundamental to who we are as people. Relationships with our loved ones, friends, romantic partners, or coworkers may be both joyful and challenging. Our ability to connect and engage with others is greatly influenced by our emotions. Using emotional intelligence to foster wholesome relationships, communicate clearly, and settle disputes is part of the alchemy of connection.

The alchemist's method of connecting is changing negative emotions into positive ones, such as exchanging resentment for forgiveness, resentment for compassion, and empathy for jealousy. By doing this, we may foster an atmosphere of harmony and positivity for both ourselves and those around us.

The Art of Emotional Alchemy: Turning Negative Feelings into Positive Energy

Effective communication is one of the most important aspects of creating good connections. In order to effectively communicate, we must not only express ourselves but also listen carefully to others. Effective communication may foster an environment of trust and understanding that can make our relationships stronger.

Constructive dispute resolution is another element of creating strong connections. Any relationship will inevitably have conflict, but how we handle it can have a big impact. The alchemist's method of handling conflicts includes accepting our feelings and using them to lead us in the right direction. We can utilise empathy and understanding to discover common ground and progress towards resolution rather than criticising others or avoiding the issue.

We must also develop self-awareness and emotional control if we want to create healthy partnerships. Understanding our own emotions and triggers helps us

The Art of Emotional Alchemy: Turning Negative Feelings into Positive Energy

better control them and avert conflict. We can comprehend others and respond to their needs correctly by using our emotional intelligence.

Having healthy relationships in our life can have a huge impact on how happy, supportive, and personally developed we are. It's crucial to keep in mind nevertheless that creating solid friendships takes time and effort. We must be willing to make an investment in our relationships and engage in honest and open communication.

According to the alchemist Paulo Coelho, "When we are in love, we always endeavour to improve. Everything around us improves as we work to become better than we are." We may change our relationships into sources of love, support, and growth by harnessing the alchemy of connection.

The Art of Emotional Alchemy: Turning Negative Feelings into Positive Energy

Take the following as an example. Maria and John had two kids together after ten years of marriage. But, as a result of parental duties, work stress, and unaddressed issues, their relationship had grown strained over time. Maria and John began to fight more frequently and felt estranged from one another.

Maria made the decision to change their relationship through the alchemy of connection. She started by using "I" statements rather than blaming John to convey her emotions in a direct and nonjudgmental manner. She also made a point of listening intently to John's perspective and comprehending it.

Maria and John were able to resolve their issues and mend their relationship via direct and honest conversation. Also, they began setting a high priority on spending time together and cultivating thankfulness for one another's contributions to the family.

The Art of Emotional Alchemy: Turning Negative Feelings into Positive Energy

Their bond grew stronger and more gratifying over time, leading to happier and more fruitful lives for both of them.

To sum up, the alchemy of connection entails utilising emotional intelligence to build strong bonds with others and communicate clearly. We may cultivate an environment that is peaceful and fulfilling for everyone around us and for ourselves by learning to shift unpleasant emotions into positive ones and by exercising empathy, understanding, and self-awareness.

Although it takes time and effort to develop good relationships, the rewards are enormous. Rumi, an alchemist, once stated, "I started hunting for you as soon as I learned of my first love, not realising how foolish that was. Nowhere does a couple eventually find each other. They have always been with each other." We can make all of our connections into sources of love and support by applying the alchemy of connection.

The Art of Emotional Alchemy: Turning Negative Feelings into Positive Energy

The Alchemy of Self-Discovery: Exploring Your Inner World

The voyage of self-discovery may be thrilling and difficult. It entails examining your inner world, comprehending your emotions, and becoming more self-aware. Self-discovery is a process that takes time, patience, and self-compassion because it can reveal difficult feelings and realities. It is also a process that can help you grow personally, get more self-acceptance, and live a more fulfilling life.

Turning inward and delving into the depths of your psyche are essential steps in the alchemy of self-discovery. It's like setting off on an inner journey to the centre of who you are, searching for hidden gems and bringing to light aspects of yourself that have been shrouded in mystery. Although we may have been avoiding or denying certain elements of ourselves, this process is not always simple.

The Art of Emotional Alchemy: Turning Negative Feelings into Positive Energy

Self-awareness is a crucial component of self-discovery. Knowing and comprehending your own ideas, feelings, and behaviours entails this. We may recognise our patterns and inclinations, comprehend our strengths and shortcomings, and make more informed decisions in life when we are self-aware.

Self-acceptance is a key component of self-discovery. This entails accepting every facet of who you are, even the demanding or unpleasant qualities. Realising your complexity and diversity as a human being—and the importance of each and every one of your experiences and feelings—is key.

The alchemy of self-discovery also entails developing an openness and feeling of curiosity. This entails being open to learning about yourself and the world around you as well as being willing to explore new concepts, viewpoints, and experiences.

The Art of Emotional Alchemy: Turning Negative Feelings into Positive Energy

It also entails being open to challenging yourself to change and grow by challenging your assumptions and ideas.

Starting a journal is one method to get the process of self-discovery started. You can gain more self-awareness and create a safe environment for you to explore your emotions and inner world by writing down your thoughts, feelings, and experiences. Through meditation or mindfulness exercises, you can connect with your inner self and develop a sense of presence and quiet as another approach to explore who you are.

In order to discover oneself, one must actively seek out new challenges and experiences. This could entail visiting new locations, taking part in novel pursuits, or discovering novel hobbies. We can learn new things about ourselves and have a deeper grasp of what makes us function when we venture outside of our comfort zones and try new things.

The Art of Emotional Alchemy: Turning Negative Feelings into Positive Energy

The alchemy of self-discovery is ultimately about accepting the process of growing more completely into who we are. It's about realising that we change and evolve constantly and that the process of self-discovery never truly ends. Rumi, a poet, once remarked "I thought the world needed to change yesterday because I was smart. Now that I am wiser, I am changing."

The fascinating contradiction is that when I accept myself exactly as I am, then I can change, said psychologist Carl Rogers. Self-discovery does not involve striving to change or improve ourselves; rather, it entails accepting and appreciating all aspects of who we are and using this understanding to guide our decisions.

It is crucial to keep in mind that self-discovery is an ongoing process as you go forwards. It's never too late to learn more about who you are because your inner landscape is always morphing and developing.

The Art of Emotional Alchemy: Turning Negative Feelings into Positive Energy

Be kind to yourself while you explore your inner world, and be curious and open to your discoveries. Never forget that there is no one "correct" way to be; instead, embrace your special traits and personality as an integral part of your path.

Self-care is a fundamental component of self-discovery. In order to have a happy and fulfilled life, it is essential to take care of your physical, emotional, and mental health. Exercise, meditation, therapy, and spending time in nature are some examples of such practices. It could also entail establishing sound limits and placing your own needs first.

The process of self-discovery is ultimately about loving and accepting yourself. You have the ability to change your inner world into one of happiness, tranquilly, and contentment, just as the alchemist does when turning base metals into gold.

The Art of Emotional Alchemy: Turning Negative Feelings into Positive Energy

Remember the wise words of novelist and activist Audre Lorde as you embrace your individual journey: "Taking care of myself is not self-indulgence; it is self-preservation, and that is an act of political warfare." You are committing a potent act of self-love and development by making the time to contemplate your inner world and give yourself the attention they deserve.

*

The Art of Emotional Alchemy: Turning Negative Feelings into Positive Energy

The Alchemist's Legacy: Leaving a Positive Emotional Footprint

The legacy we leave behind reflects the difference we have made in the world, and it extends beyond the things we own and the things we accomplish during our lifetime. Our emotional imprint, the emotions we caused in others, and the memories we leave behind all have an impact on our legacy. The heritage of the alchemist is about creating emotional healing for everyone, not just for ourselves. It's about changing the world for the better, one person at a time.

It takes conscious effort to behave with kindness, compassion, and understanding towards others in order to leave a positive emotional footprint. It involves being aware of our behaviour and how it impacts those around us.

The Art of Emotional Alchemy: Turning Negative Feelings into Positive Energy

We can have a positive influence on the people in our lives and leave a lasting legacy of love and goodness by being aware of our emotions and skilfully controlling them.

Acts of kindness are one method to leave a positive emotional footprint. Even modest deeds of kindness can make a big difference in the lives of those around us. Whether it's lending a sympathetic ear to a buddy in need or offering assistance to a complete stranger, deeds of kindness can contribute to spreading happiness throughout the world. According to the proverbial saying attributed to Aesop, "No act of kindness, no matter how tiny, is ever wasted."

The relationships we foster have a significant role in creating a positive emotional legacy. People's perceptions of us and the memories they associate with us can be greatly influenced by the way we engage with them. Being open, truthful, and vulnerable is necessary

The Art of Emotional Alchemy: Turning Negative Feelings into Positive Energy

for establishing healthy relationships. It demands us to be present with the people we care about and to communicate effectively. We may leave a lasting legacy of love and goodness by cultivating our relationships with others that will last long after we are gone.

The legacy of the alchemist ultimately revolves around leading a life that is meaningful and purposeful. It's about realising the value of emotional wellness and how it may have a beneficial influence on the world. It's about leaving behind a lasting emotional impression that reflects our ideals and the difference we've made in the lives of the people we cherish.

People will forget what you said and what you did, but they won't forget how you made them feel, as Maya Angelou famously put it. The alchemist's legacy is about making a positive, loving, and kind impression on the people in our lives that will endure a lifetime.

The Art of Emotional Alchemy: Turning Negative Feelings into Positive Energy

We may leave a legacy that will motivate and uplift future generations by embracing the concepts of emotional wellbeing.

*

The Art of Emotional Alchemy: Turning Negative Feelings into Positive Energy

The Alchemy of Courage: Transforming Fear into Bravery

It's possible for fear to make you paralysed. It may prevent you from going after your goals, attempting new things, or even from living your life to the fullest. But, fear is also a healthy feeling that guides us through life and keeps us safe. The secret to overcoming fear is to understand how to turn it into courage rather than trying to get rid of it. We will examine the alchemy of courage in this chapter and how to apply it to transform your fear into bravery.

The Courage to Confront Your Fears

"Courage doesn't yell all the time. Sometimes having the quiet confidence to declare, "I'll try again tomorrow" at the end of the day displays courage. (Mary Anne Radmacher)

The Art of Emotional Alchemy: Turning Negative Feelings into Positive Energy

Recognizing and facing your concerns is the first step to converting fear into bravery. This process can be challenging and uncomfortable, and it requires guts. But, facing your concerns head-on is the only way to get over them.

The ability to face fear is what defines courage rather than the absence of dread. It is normal to wish to flee or steer clear of the source of your fear when you are frightened. Nevertheless, doing so just feeds the cycle of dread and increases its hold over you.

Instead, make an effort to face your fear gradually. This could entail taking little chances, engaging in self-compassion exercises, and reminding oneself that fear is a healthy emotion. The more you confront your concerns, the less difficult it is to get through them.

The Art of Emotional Alchemy: Turning Negative Feelings into Positive Energy

The Willingness to Act

"Life grows or shrinks according to one's courage."
(Anas Nin)

After facing your concerns, the next thing to do is to act. Being courageous involves acting in spite of your concerns as well as being fearless. This could entail putting yourself in uncomfortable situations, experimenting, and taking chances.

Taking initiative might be frightening, but it also gives you power. It enables you to advance personally and allows you to strengthen your self-assurance and resilience. It's crucial to keep in mind that taking action doesn't require you to be flawless or possess all the knowledge. Sometimes just attempting can have a positive impact.

The Art of Emotional Alchemy: Turning Negative Feelings into Positive Energy

The Courage to Struggle

"Success is not definitive, failure is not fatal: what counts is the fortitude to go on." —William Churchill

There will be moments when you experience setbacks and difficulties, even after you have faced your anxieties and taken action. The ability to persevere is essential for getting beyond these challenges. This entails persevering through difficulties and pushing forwards in spite of failures and setbacks.

Resilience, tenacity, and a positive outlook are necessary for persistence. It is about making amends for your errors, adjusting to change, and remaining goal-focused. It's crucial to keep in mind that setbacks and failures are a normal part of learning and can offer insightful information and chances for development.

The Art of Emotional Alchemy: Turning Negative Feelings into Positive Energy

The Courage to Be Vulnerable

"Vulnerability is having the guts to show up and be seen when we have no control over the outcome; it is not winning or losing." Brene Brown

The ability to be vulnerable is also a necessary component of the alchemy of courage. Although it is frequently mistaken for a sign of weakness, vulnerability actually indicates strength. Being open and vulnerable requires courage since it exposes you to the prospect of rejection or criticism.

Vulnerability, however, also promotes genuine connections and partnerships. It enables stronger interpersonal connections, the sharing of feelings and experiences, and mutual learning.

Self-compassion and self-acceptance practices are essential for being vulnerable.

The Art of Emotional Alchemy: Turning Negative Feelings into Positive Energy

This entails accepting your deservingness of love and connection despite your shortcomings and imperfections.

"Courage is not the absence of fear, but the triumph over it. The brave man is not he who does not feel afraid, but he who conquers that fear." Nelson Mandela

Practice embracing our fears is one method to turn fear into bravery. Little measures can be taken to do this, gradually boosting our self-assurance and resiliency. For instance, if we're afraid of public speaking, we can start by speaking out in informal settings or offering to present to a small group of people we know. The complexity of the situations we face can be gradually increased as we gain comfort until we are able to confront our anxiety head-on.

Focusing on our ideals and objectives is another method for developing courage. We are more likely to be inspired to take risks and face our concerns when we

The Art of Emotional Alchemy: Turning Negative Feelings into Positive Energy

have a clear sense of purpose and direction. Setting objectives that are consistent with our values entails pausing to consider our values and what is significant to us.

While we face our worries, it is crucial to exercise self-compassion. We must be kind to ourselves and recognise that it's normal to experience fear or anxiety. This entails identifying our inner critic and developing the ability to combat negative self-talk. We may give ourselves the support and inspiration we need to face our fears with courage and resilience by engaging in self-compassion practices.

The process of turning fear into bravery is comparable to transmutation in the alchemical sense. We can transform our fear into courage through the process of self-discovery, introspection, and transformation, just as alchemists attempted to turn lead into gold.

The Art of Emotional Alchemy: Turning Negative Feelings into Positive Energy

The alchemy of courage is a formidable instrument for converting fear into bravery, to sum up. We may increase our courage and resiliency by accepting fear and using it as a springboard for progress. Although the path to courage is not simple, it is eventually beneficial since it enables us to go over challenges and accomplish our objectives.

"Vulnerability is not weakness; it's our greatest measure of courage," writes author Brene Brown. We can find our inner strength and feel empowered when we allow ourselves to be open and vulnerable and face our anxieties. Through developing bravery, we can leave our comfort zones and accomplish things that seemed unattainable at first.

So let's take a brave stance towards life and confront our worries. Let's not forget that bravery is not the absence of fear, but rather the readiness to face it head-on. According to Albert Camus, "I discovered that even

The Art of Emotional Alchemy: Turning Negative Feelings into Positive Energy

though it was winter, I had an unstoppable summer within me. And I'm glad about that. Because it asserts that no matter how strongly the outside world pulls against me, I have something better and stronger pushing back."

*

The Art of Emotional Alchemy: Turning Negative Feelings into Positive Energy

The Alchemy of Resilience: Bouncing Back from Emotional Setbacks

Life has many unexpected changes and twists that can emotionally exhaust and overwhelm us. These setbacks, which can range from the death of a loved one to a significant life change, can be challenging to handle and put our emotional fortitude to the test. But, with the power of inner alchemy, we can learn how to develop from these experiences and become more resilient than ever before.

Understanding how to deal with and adjust to life's adversities is essential to the alchemy of resilience. It's about acquiring the mental tenacity and emotional stamina necessary to confront adversity head-on and come out on the other side with renewed strength and a sense of direction.

The Art of Emotional Alchemy: Turning Negative Feelings into Positive Energy

Deep self-awareness, a readiness to learn from our mistakes, and the capacity to exercise self-compassion in the face of difficulties are all necessary for this.

Creating a growth mindset is a crucial component of gaining resilience. We may reframe losses as opportunities for growth and learning rather than seeing them as failures. According to author and researcher Carol Dweck, "Challenges are thrilling rather than terrifying when you have a development mentality. So rather than thinking, 'oh, I'm going to show my shortcomings', you say, 'Wow, here's a chance to grow'."

The capacity for self-care is a crucial component of resilience. This entails regularly attending to our bodily, emotional, and mental well-being. This can involve doing regular exercise, maintaining a nutritious diet, getting enough rest, and taking part in enjoyable and relaxing activities.

The Art of Emotional Alchemy: Turning Negative Feelings into Positive Energy

Building resilience can also benefit from creating a network of friends and family who are encouraging. We can feel more resilient and be better prepared to tackle challenges when we have individuals we can turn to for support and encouragement.

It's critical to keep in mind that developing resilience is a continuous process of growth and development. We may build the resilience we require to deal with life's ups and downs by adopting a growth mindset, engaging in self-care, and fostering our relationships.

According to Maya Angelou, "Even though you may suffer numerous setbacks, you must not give up. In fact, it could be essential to experience failure in order to understand who you are, what you can rise from, and how you can still overcome it."

The lives of people who have overcome enormous obstacles and are now stronger are examples of the

The Art of Emotional Alchemy: Turning Negative Feelings into Positive Energy

alchemy of resilience. Nelson Mandela, who served 27 years in jail for his anti-apartheid activities, came out of it with a profound feeling of compassion and forgiveness, and he has devoted the rest of his life to advancing peace and reconciliation. Similar to how J.K. Rowling has discussed how her challenges ultimately made her a greater writer and person, Rowling endured countless rejections before finally publishing the Harry Potter books.

In conclusion, the alchemy of resilience entails converting obstacles into chances for development and education. We may build the mental toughness and emotional fortitude we need to overcome adversity and come out stronger than before by adopting a growth mindset, engaging in self-care, and prioritising our relationships.

*

The Art of Emotional Alchemy: Turning Negative Feelings into Positive Energy

The Alchemist's Canvas: Painting Your Emotional Landscape

We all work as painters as people, sculpting our emotional environment with each and every thought, emotion, and deed. We utilise our minds and bodies to produce a singular work of emotion, much like a painter who uses a canvas to convey their deepest ideas and feelings.

We are not always in charge of the colours and shapes that appear on our canvas, however, unlike a painter. External influences including our surroundings, relationships, and past experiences frequently alter our emotional landscape. This may result in a canvas that is disorganised and chaotic, with clashing hues and disorganised shapes.

Being a mindful and intentional artist is essential for producing beautiful emotional landscapes. We must

The Art of Emotional Alchemy: Turning Negative Feelings into Positive Energy

develop the ability to manage our brushstrokes and select the colours that best convey our ideas. By doing this, we can produce a work of art that not only captures the eye but also conveys our deepest aspirations and principles.

Understanding the various emotions that make up our canvas is one of the first stages to being a conscious artist. We have a palette of emotions to choose from, much like a painter has a variety of colours to choose from. While some of these emotions are uplifting and upbeat, others are depressing and depleting.

We can better understand our own emotional landscape by learning to recognise and categorise our feelings. The ability to detect and control our own emotions as well as the emotions of others is known as emotional intelligence, and its base is self-awareness.

By becoming more self-aware, we can start deliberately picking the emotions we wish to portray on our canvas.

The Art of Emotional Alchemy: Turning Negative Feelings into Positive Energy

To achieve a harmonic and balanced emotional environment, we must learn the art of managing our thoughts and emotions.

Mindfulness is one of the best methods for controlling our emotions. Being mindful is practising being fully aware of our thoughts, feelings, and bodily sensations in the present moment. By engaging in mindfulness exercises, we can learn to examine our emotions objectively, which enables us to react to them more purposefully and successfully.

Self-compassion is another strategy for controlling our emotions. The act of treating oneself with kindness, acceptance, and understanding is known as self-compassion. We can lessen negative emotions like shame, guilt, and self-criticism, which are frequently the cause of emotional unrest, by practising self-compassion.

The Art of Emotional Alchemy: Turning Negative Feelings into Positive Energy

Furthermore, it's critical to keep in mind that building a wonderful emotional environment is a continuous process. It is a continuous process that calls for perseverance, practice, and patience. We must continually work on our emotional landscape, honing our brushstrokes and selecting our colours with care, just like a painter who must constantly practise their profession.

We will surely encounter difficulties and obstacles as we advance in our development as conscious artists. But with every challenge, we have the chance to learn and develop, to hone our skill and build a more lovely emotional landscape.

Vincent van Gogh, a well-known painter, once said, "I am seeking, I am struggling, and I am in it with all of my heart."

*

The Art of Emotional Alchemy: Turning Negative Feelings into Positive Energy

The Alchemy of Patience: Navigating Your Emotions with Grace

Life's journey can be difficult, and our emotions can frequently feel overpowering. It's simple to get lost in the tumult of our emotions and overlook our objectives. But, mastering the art of patience might enable us to handle our feelings gracefully and maintain our attention on what's important.

We must learn to be patient with our emotional journey, just like the alchemist who patiently waits for their components to change into gold. Emotions are not constant; they fluctuate like the tide, and occasionally we must wait for the storm to pass before the sun may shine once more.

Self-awareness and the capacity to disengage from our emotions and observe them objectively are necessary for patience. Although we have no control over our

The Art of Emotional Alchemy: Turning Negative Feelings into Positive Energy

sentiments, we do have influence over how we deal with them. We can develop the ability to respond with grace and patience rather than impulsively.

We can see the wider picture when we have patience. We may enjoy the ride with all of its highs and lows and have faith that everything occurs for a reason. Patience enables us to develop and learn from all of our experiences, including the difficult ones, and makes us stronger in the face of difficulty.

The alchemist must have trust in the process as they wait for their transformation to take place. In a similar vein, we must trust that our emotional journey will take us to the right place. We must have faith in our own resiliency and capacity to go over any challenge.

It is not necessary to stifle or completely shun our emotions in order to practise patience alchemy. Giving them the time and space they require to change means

The Art of Emotional Alchemy: Turning Negative Feelings into Positive Energy

truly loving them. By exercising patience, we can change our feelings into something lovely, much as an alchemist may change base metals into gold.

"Patience is the virtue that permits us to tolerate suffering, hardship, and adversity with tranquillity and without complaint," Thomas Aquinas, a prominent philosopher and theologian, once stated. We can come out on the other side more resilient and stronger if we can patiently suffer our emotional failures.

Ultimately, learning the alchemy of patience can teach us how to handle our emotions with grace and fortitude. It necessitates self-awareness, faith, and the patience to wait for change to happen. As the alchemist turns base metals into gold, so too can we transform our emotions into something lovely and useful by learning to be patient. We can weather any storm and come out stronger on the other side if we have patience and keep in mind that everything happens in its own time.

The Art of Emotional Alchemy: Turning Negative Feelings into Positive Energy

The Alchemy of Humility: Letting Go of Negative Emotions

Alchemy is not just about turning base metals into gold; it also involves turning negative emotions in the human mind into good ones. Humility is a crucial component of this development. When we are humble, we are able to let go of unfavourable feelings like resentment, envy, and rage that would otherwise consume us and prevent us from finding happiness and peace.

Being humble is a show of strength rather than weakness. Admitting our errors, accepting help from others, and admitting our inadequacies all require guts. We become more open to development and change when we let go of our arrogance and ego. We become more open to education and consciousness expansion.

We can develop empathy and compassion for others by being humble. We become more understanding of others'

The Art of Emotional Alchemy: Turning Negative Feelings into Positive Energy

troubles and are less prone to judge them when we are aware of our own flaws and struggles. We become more tolerant and compassionate towards those who are in need.

Understanding our limitations and embracing our humanity are key components of the alchemy of humility. It entails realising that we are fallible and that making mistakes is a necessary element of learning. We become more flexible to change and better equipped to handle setbacks and failures when we adopt a modest mindset.

Lao Tzu's wise words best capture the essence of humility: "Walk with them as you lead others. The best leaders are invisible to the general public. The people revere and praise the second-best. People will fear the next thing, then they will detest it. When the work of the best leader is complete, the people exclaim, "We did it ourselves!""

The Art of Emotional Alchemy: Turning Negative Feelings into Positive Energy

Living in the present and appreciating the little things in life are both made possible by humility. We become more pleased with what we have and are less prone to compare ourselves to others when we let go of our attachment to material belongings and societal status.

We can begin the alchemy of humility by admitting and accepting our flaws and limits. Also, we can practise appreciation and thankfulness for the people and things in our lives. When dealing with people, we can exercise active listening and open-mindedness and avoid passing judgement or criticism on them. Ultimately, we can concentrate on replacing resentment, anger, and other unpleasant emotions with compassion, forgiveness, and kindness.

Letting go of unfavourable feelings and accepting that we are all fallible human beings who make mistakes is the act of humility. It necessitates embracing criticism, owning up to our mistakes, and working to become

The Art of Emotional Alchemy: Turning Negative Feelings into Positive Energy

better people. By engaging in acts of humility, we make room for development and improvement.

I've learned that people will forget what you said and what you did, but they won't forget how you made them feel, as the eminent novelist Maya Angelou put it. This quotation emphasises the value of humility since the people we interact with might be affected by our words and deeds for a long time. We are more likely to make a good impression on people when we let go of negative feelings and approach problems with humility.

Consider a situation where a mistake is made by a teammate that has a detrimental effect on a project you are both working on. You might respond indignantly and accusatory, which would almost certainly result in tension and a breakdown in communication. Yet, if you approach the matter with humility, you might admit that slip-ups occur and enquire as to how you can cooperate to resolve the problem.

The Art of Emotional Alchemy: Turning Negative Feelings into Positive Energy

In this situation, showing humility would help you and your teammate develop a stronger working connection and open the door to constructive change. Also, it would show that you are eager to work with others and learn from your mistakes, which would ultimately lead to success.

In the alchemy of converting bad emotions into positive ones, humility is a key component. Humility increases our capacity for development, adaptation, and learning. We develop greater empathy and compassion for other people, a sense of gratitude for what we already have, and improved coping skills for life's difficulties. Humility, in the words of the renowned philosopher Confucius, "is the foundation of all virtues."

*

The Art of Emotional Alchemy: Turning Negative Feelings into Positive Energy

The Alchemy of Trust: Building Trust with Yourself and Others

All healthy relationships, both with ourselves and others, are built on trust. It is what enables us to feel connected to the people and things that are important to us as well as protected and secure. But, developing trust may be a delicate and challenging process that calls for perseverance, openness, and a willingness to take chances. In this chapter, we'll look at the chemistry of trust and how to foster it in both our personal and professional relationships.

Self-confidence, or the conviction that we are capable, competent, and deserving of our own love and respect, is the foundation of trust. We can make decisions, establish healthy boundaries, and take risks that are consistent with our beliefs and objectives when we have faith in ourselves.

The Art of Emotional Alchemy: Turning Negative Feelings into Positive Energy

But if we don't believe in ourselves, we could experience self-doubt, uncertainty, and a lack of purpose in life.

We must be willing to respect our feelings, pay attention to our intuition, and accept responsibility for our decisions if we want to develop self-trust. We may get started by being kind to ourselves, recognising our accomplishments, and taking lessons from our missteps. When we believe in ourselves, we are more likely to draw in companions and circumstances that reflect our true selves.

Vulnerability and the readiness to run emotional risks are necessary for trust in others. Even though we may have experienced pain or betrayal in the past, clinging to those memories can keep us from making new friends or having new experiences. We must let go of the past and be present in the present if we are to learn to trust again. In the end, it necessitates that we extend others the benefit of the doubt and have faith in their ability to

The Art of Emotional Alchemy: Turning Negative Feelings into Positive Energy

develop and change, even though it may include establishing boundaries and making our requirements known.

By acting and behaving consistently throughout time, trust can be built. Little acts of generosity, truthfulness, and dependability can strengthen our relationships, yet betrayals can cause that trust to fall apart swiftly. It's crucial to be willing to listen to and learn from the viewpoints of the people in our lives and to interact with them in an open and honest manner.

The alchemy of trust entails the conversion of fear into faith, ambiguity into connection, and scepticism into assurance. It necessitates a readiness to be open to emotional risk, a desire to be vulnerable, and a belief in both oneself and others. Building trust in ourselves and our relationships lays the groundwork for development, resiliency, and deep connections.

The Art of Emotional Alchemy: Turning Negative Feelings into Positive Energy

"Life is held together by trust. It is the single most important component of good communication. It serves as the underlying tenet of all interactions." Steven Covey

We develop a positive outlook and learn to appreciate the wealth of life via the alchemy of gratitude. We learn to transform unfavourable feelings into love, the universe's most potent energy, through the alchemy of love. We discover how to control our emotions for creative inspiration and self-expression through the alchemy of creativity. We create satisfying connections that enrich our lives through the alchemy of connection. The alchemy of self-discovery allows us to delve into our inner selves and discover our genuine potential.

We can overcome our fear through the alchemy of courage, and we can overcome our emotional defeats through the alchemy of resilience. The alchemy of humility helps us let go of negative feelings, while the

The Art of Emotional Alchemy: Turning Negative Feelings into Positive Energy

alchemy of trust helps us establish trust with both ourselves and other people.

In conclusion, although the path of emotional alchemy is challenging, it is also fruitful. It takes time, courage, and self-awareness to transform negative emotions into positive ones. It takes us to face our inner demons and muster the courage to turn them into sources of motivation and personal development.

*

The Art of Emotional Alchemy: Turning Negative Feelings into Positive Energy

The Alchemy of Wisdom: Learning from Your Emotions

The alchemy of knowledge entails comprehending and taking lessons from our feelings. We can think of emotions as teachers who teach us important things about ourselves, other people, and the outside world. We may improve our awareness of ourselves and others, as well as our ability for empathy, compassion, and connection, by being receptive to the wisdom that emotions have to offer.

Developing the capacity to recognise and consider our emotions is a crucial component of the alchemy of wisdom. This entails stepping back from the intensity of our emotions and looking at them really and compassionately. By doing this, we can learn more about the underlying values, wants, and beliefs that motivate our emotional reactions.

The Art of Emotional Alchemy: Turning Negative Feelings into Positive Energy

Using our emotions as a source of inspiration and direction is a crucial component of the alchemy of knowledge. We can use emotions to determine what is genuinely important to us and to discover the inspiration and bravery to go for our objectives. As we connect with our most fundamental beliefs and goals, emotions can also give us a feeling of purpose and meaning.

It's crucial to develop an attitude of humility and openness if you want to completely benefit from the alchemy of wisdom. This entails being open to learning from others as well as from our own errors and shortcomings, as well as being willing to admit when we don't know something. It also entails understanding that there is always more to understand and learn about ourselves and the world around us, and that our emotions are only one aspect of the bigger picture.

What lies behind us and what lies before us are insignificant matters in comparison to what lies within

The Art of Emotional Alchemy: Turning Negative Feelings into Positive Energy

us, according to American poet and philosopher Ralph Waldo Emerson. We may use our emotions as potent weapons for personal development and transformation when we cultivate the alchemy of wisdom because it allows us to draw from the limitless reservoir of knowledge that exists within us.

The experience of a woman by the name of Sarah is one illustration of the alchemy of wisdom in action. Sarah had always experienced worry and self-doubt, and she frequently caught herself in destructive thought patterns that made her feel helpless and stuck. Sarah, though, started to view her emotions differently after years of treatment and introspection. She came to see that her nervousness was frequently a sign that she was putting others' needs before her own, and that her self-doubt was a result of a deep-seated fear of failing and being rejected.

The Art of Emotional Alchemy: Turning Negative Feelings into Positive Energy

Sarah started to make changes in her life that were more in line with her genuine wants and aspirations when she was able to recognise the underlying ideas and values that were motivating her behaviour via her examination of her emotions. She began prioritising her own needs, establishing boundaries with others, and pursuing her creative interests. Sarah was able to get over her fear and self-doubt and live a more contented and meaningful life as she gained a strong sense of faith in herself and her own understanding.

In conclusion, the alchemy of wisdom entails harnessing our emotions as a source of inspiration and direction while also learning from them. We can access the limitless store of knowledge that resides within us by cultivating humility, openness, and curiosity. We can also employ our emotions as potent instruments for personal development and transformation. "The odd paradox is that when I accept myself precisely as I am, then I can change," American psychologist Carl Rogers famously

The Art of Emotional Alchemy: Turning Negative Feelings into Positive Energy

said. We foster the circumstances for profound and long-lasting change when we approach our emotions with curiosity and compassion.

*

The Art of Emotional Alchemy: Turning Negative Feelings into Positive Energy

The Alchemy of Balance: Finding Equilibrium in Your Emotions

Like ocean waves, emotions can fluctuate frequently. Similar to how the moon's gravitational pull affects the tides, both internal and external influences, including our thoughts, beliefs, and experiences, have an impact on how we feel. Although it can be difficult, maintaining emotional balance is essential for our general wellbeing and happiness.

Too much emotion might cause us to feel overwhelmed, receptive, and out of control. On the other hand, repressing or ignoring our emotions can result in numbness, a sense of being cut off from the world, and internal conflict. Learning to surf the waves of our emotions while remaining calm and grounded is the secret to achieving emotional equilibrium.

The Art of Emotional Alchemy: Turning Negative Feelings into Positive Energy

We have to maintain our balance in the face of ever-changing emotions, much like a tightrope walker. These are some methods to assist you in achieving emotional balance:

Develop mindfulness

Being present and non-judgmentally aware of your thoughts, emotions, and sensations is the practice of mindfulness. It entails becoming aware of and compassionately examining your inner experience. You can become more aware of your emotional states, spot patterns, and react with more clarity and intention by practising mindfulness.

Develop Self-Compassion

When faced with difficulties or failure, self-compassion is the act of treating oneself with care and understanding. It entails warmly and without judgement accepting your

The Art of Emotional Alchemy: Turning Negative Feelings into Positive Energy

flaws and difficulties. You can calm your emotional turmoil and prevent yourself from engaging in self-blame or negative self-talk by practising self-compassion.

Engage in Self-Care

The act of looking after your physical, emotional, and mental health is known as self-care. It entails doing things for yourself that nourish and support you, including working out, eating well, meditating, or spending time in nature. You can refuel your energy, lower your stress level, and improve your emotional resiliency by making self-care a priority.

Seek Assistance

Finding balance in your emotional life can be achieved by asking for support from others. Reaching out for assistance can give you a safe space to express your

The Art of Emotional Alchemy: Turning Negative Feelings into Positive Energy

thoughts, get perspective, and get advice, whether it's by talking to a trusted friend or family member, seeing a therapist, or participating in a support group.

Lao Tzu, an ancient Chinese philosopher, once stated that nature moves slowly but efficiently. It could take some time to find emotional equilibrium, but with perseverance, practice, and self-compassion, you can develop the skill of riding the waves with more grace and ease.

Jon Kabat-Zinn, a psychotherapist and mindfulness instructor, said that while you cannot stop the waves, you can learn to surf. You can develop the skill of an experienced surfer, navigating the ups and downs with more ease, and finding joy and significance in the journey by practising emotional equilibrium.

Suppose that you are experiencing a difficult time at work. You can be experiencing stress, anxiety, and

The Art of Emotional Alchemy: Turning Negative Feelings into Positive Energy

overload due to your job and obligations. By taking a few deep breaths and focusing on the here and now, you can practise mindfulness so that you don't get sucked into these feelings. You can acknowledge that your thoughts and feelings are a normal aspect of the human experience and observe them without passing judgement. By constantly reminding yourself that you are doing the best you can in a challenging situation and that it's okay to struggle and make errors, you may also practise self-compassion. Last but not least, you can practise self-care by taking breaks, going for walks in the fresh air, or doing something that makes you happy and relaxed. By utilising these concepts, you would have already started upon the path of finding equilibrium.

We can develop the knowledge and fortitude necessary to handle life's ups and downs with grace and resiliency by alchemizing our emotions. Without passing judgement or showing opposition, we can learn to understand and value the entire range of our emotions,

The Art of Emotional Alchemy: Turning Negative Feelings into Positive Energy

from the good to the bad. In order to live a life of honesty, integrity, and alignment, we can also work to find the delicate balance between our inner and outer selves.

The alchemy of balance is a lifelong endeavour that necessitates focus, intention, and practise. In order to live a life of fullness, purpose, and joy, we must achieve emotional balance and harmony. Happiness, according to the Greek philosopher Aristotle, is the meaning and goal of life as well as the culmination of human existence.

*

<u>The Art of Emotional Alchemy: Turning Negative Feelings into Positive Energy</u>

The Alchemy of Self-Love: Transforming Negative Self-Talk into Self-Love.

The basis of emotional health is self-love. It is the act of treating oneself with acceptance, kindness, and compassion. Thoughts of unworthiness, self-doubt, and even self-sabotage can result from the negative self-talk we frequently indulge in. The good news is that, like any other ability, self-love can be developed with practice. Positive self-talk may be changed into self-love with the correct attitude, resources, and practices, and we can develop a positive, fulfilling connection with ourselves.

Becoming conscious of our habitual negative self-talk is the first step in developing self-love. We may not even be aware of these patterns because they are frequently deeply ingrained in our thinking. These may manifest as severe self-judgement, self-doubt, or critical thoughts. Once we are aware of these patterns, we can start to

The Art of Emotional Alchemy: Turning Negative Feelings into Positive Energy

confront them and switch out negative thoughts with positive ones.

Self-compassion is a potent strategy for changing negative self-talk. The act of treating oneself with the same consideration, kindness, and support that we would extend to a good friend is known as self-compassion. We can start to interrupt the cycle of negative self-talk and develop a more adoring and caring relationship with ourselves by showing compassion to ourselves.

Gratitude is a strong tool for developing self-love. We can turn our attention from our flaws and failings to our strengths and positive traits by concentrating on what we like about ourselves. When we practise self-gratitude, we are more likely to be kind to ourselves, treat ourselves with care, and make decisions that promote our wellbeing.

The Art of Emotional Alchemy: Turning Negative Feelings into Positive Energy

It's crucial to keep in mind that practising self-love doesn't require perfection or having everything together. It's about treating yourself with respect and compassion and accepting yourself as you are, warts and all. To love oneself is the start of a lifetime relationship, as the philosopher Aristotle once stated. When we accept and love ourselves, we let a world of opportunity and potential in.

Setting appropriate limits and taking care of our physical, emotional, and mental well-being are other aspects of practising self-love. It entails putting our own wellbeing first and saying no to requests that don't serve us. It entails allowing oneself to relax, have fun, and play. We build a solid and empowering foundation for all facets of our lives when we love and respect ourselves.

It may take some time and work to change our negative self-talk patterns and the path to self-love.

The Art of Emotional Alchemy: Turning Negative Feelings into Positive Energy

Yet if we are persistent, committed, and compassionate towards ourselves, we can change our connection with ourselves and build a life that is joyful, loving, and fulfilling.

"Your duty is not to seek for love, but just to explore and find all the obstacles within yourself that you have created against it," the eminent poet and philosopher Rumi once said. We can see a significant change in our life and the world around us by removing those obstacles and practising self-love. So let's resolve to cultivate self-love and, in doing so, fully realise the power of our emotional alchemy.

Start by speaking to yourself with kindness and compassion to develop self-love. Prioritise your needs and practise self-care. Forgive yourself for previous transgressions and acknowledge that you are making the best use of your resources.

The Art of Emotional Alchemy: Turning Negative Feelings into Positive Energy

Recall that loving oneself is not being selfish. It is essential to our general health and enables us to present our best selves to others.

Keep in mind the words of the great philosopher Aristotle as you proceed on your journey of self-love: "To love oneself is the beginning of a lifelong relationship." May you have a happy, kind, and accepting relationship with yourself for the rest of your life.

*

Printed in Great Britain
by Amazon